merely Christianity

merely Christianity
A Systemic Critique of Theology

Robert M. Price

Pitchstone Publishing
Durham, North Carolina

Pitchstone Publishing
Durham, North Carolina
www.pitchstonebooks.com

Library of Congress Cataloging-in-Publication Data

Names: Price, Robert M., 1954- author.
Title: Merely Christianity : a systemic critique of theology / Robert M.
    Price.
Description: Durham, North Carolina : Pitchstone Publishing, [2022] |
    Includes bibliographical references. | Summary: "The author scrutinizes
    the beliefs and thinking of Christian theologians and explains why he no
    longer finds that cardinal Christian claims make enough sense to
    believe"— Provided by publisher.
Identifiers: LCCN 2021028192 (print) | LCCN 2021028193 (ebook) | ISBN
    9781634312219 (paperback) | ISBN 9781634312226 (ebook)
Subjects: LCSH: Christianity—Miscellanea. | Theology—Miscellanea.
Classification: LCC BR124 .P75 2022 (print) | LCC BR124 (ebook) | DDC
    230—dc23
LC record available at https://lccn.loc.gov/2021028192
LC ebook record available at https://lccn.loc.gov/2021028193

Dedicated to my friend and benefactor,
Julian Haydon.
When I grow up, I want to be just like him!

Contents

8 Contents

Preface

C.S. Lewis famously wrote: "I am not asking anyone to accept Christianity if his best reasoning tells him that the weight of evidence is against it."[1] Yet, reading what follows in the pages of his classic of apologetics, *Mere Christianity*, one may question whether it was Lewis's best reasoning that led him to accept it and to continue defending it. Rather, I suspect he was, as all apologists are by the nature of their task, mounting the best case he could for a position embraced on other grounds. One may recall his conversion account provided in his autobiography, *Surprised by Joy*. A childhood experience of seeing a flowering currant bush had triggered a world-transforming moment of mystical transcendence which sounds rather like a Zen experience.[2] Years later his Christian conversion turned on what sounds like another moment of *Satori*: Lewis converted while riding to a zoo in his brother's motorcycle side car. "When we set out I did not believe that Jesus is the Son of God and when we reached the zoo I did."[3] I somehow doubt such an experience arises rationally or that it can be defended, even understood, that way. And in this little book I want to explain why I no longer find that cardinal Christian claims make enough sense to believe.

---

1. C.S. Lewis, *Mere Christianity* (New York: Macmillan, 1960), p. 123.

2. C.S. Lewis, *Surprised by Joy: The Shape of My Early Life* (London: Collins Fontana, 1959), pp. 18–19.

3. Lewis, *Surprised by Joy*, p. 189.

I recall how once, when my friend Clark H. Pinnock, himself a Christian theologian, wrote a comment on an essay I had written for my church newsletter, a brief piece on theories of the atonement. The essay pointed out basic problems with all of them. Clark asked why I just criticized Christian doctrines and did not try to creatively repair or reformulate them? In retrospect, I guess the answer was that I had pretty much stopped believing in them. I still held them in respect, as I do now, as part of the great Christian tradition. Indeed, in those waning days of my pastorate, my "Christian education" policy was to explain the theological tradition, making sure our young people understood it, whether they accepted it or not. It would be their own decision, and I wanted to make as sure as I could that it would be an *informed* decision. I would not take for granted that they would come off the assembly line as "good Christians." That would be manipulative. Mine was, however, a policy by no means conducive to institutional member/customer "retention." I fear I was not a good pastor.

I still feel obliged to defend Christian tenets against cheap shots aimed by snarky religion-haters who have not the patience to try to understand them. Are you really striking a blow against Christianity when you ridicule Jim Bakker or Benny Hinn? These men are clowns, sideshow freaks, barnacles on the hull of Christianity, mere parasites attached to the organism. I would rather engage in serious scrutiny of the beliefs and the thinking of genuine Christian theologians. And that is the point of this book. For the gospel proclamation is not, as is claimed, a timeless revelation from heaven, but merely Christianity.

Robert M. Price
Winter Solstice 2020

1

An Infinite Personal God

Choose One

Theologians are only doing their proper job when they try to understand and explain "God." It is almost as if they were functioning as press secretaries for the Almighty. It is generally considered a wholesome task, though there is always the chance that one may suggest some new way of understanding God that will not be received well by the faithful. This is where accusations of "heresy" may arise. Such differences of opinion are disturbing because it suggests that no one can really know anything about God for sure. If God is subject to theorizing and, worse yet, revision, well, maybe the whole thing has been cooked up by clever mortals like the ones doing the rethinking now. What I am doing in this chapter, I fear, is more obviously and immediately threatening to faith. It is to deconstruct the Judeo-Christian character called "God" by scrutinizing the possible denotations of the Hebrew word for "God," namely, *Elohim*.

Elohim: Singular or Plural?

First there's the "little" matter of the ending of the word, "—im." This is a plural ending, which would ordinarily mark the word as a plu-

11

ral. If you were talking about a *group* of deities, you would use the word "Elohim." But of course in the Bible this word is traditionally translated as singular. That is, you wouldn't say "Gods is." You'd say, "Gods are." In Hebrew, admittedly, "Elohim" could go either way, but in by far the most cases it is followed by a singular verb. Why it has a plural ending, though, remains puzzling. Some have speculated that the plural ending is meant to denote the fullness of power or majesty of a single deity. Maybe so, but I think that Joseph A. Wheless[4] may have been right: the plural is a tell-tale clue to an underlying and largely effaced Israelite polytheism. On this theory, we must picture the scribes "correcting" the texts, adjusting them in order to bring them "up to date" with a new, monotheistic orthodoxy.[5] They would have set about changing all the plural verbs to singular—only they missed some, victims of what Mark C. Goodacre[6] calls "editorial fatigue." A proofreader knows how that goes.

This all might seem purely fanciful except that there are other distinct reasons to suggest (and more than suggest) the existence of Israelite polytheism. For one thing, since "El" and "Elohim" are generic terms, it is tempting to think that the various appellations *El Elyon* ("God Most High"), *El Shaddai* ("God Almighty"), *El Olam* ("God Eternal"), etc., denote not various epithets for a single deity but rather the names of various deities. The usage would be closely analogous to Baal Melkart, Aleyan Baal, Baal Peor, Baal Shalisha, and Baal Zebub, all different gods, "Baal" meaning "Lord," equally applicable to all.

4. Joseph A. Wheless, *Is it God's Word? An Exposition of the Fables and Mythology of the Bible and of the Impostures of Theology* (New York: Alfred A. Knopf, 1926), pp. 202–203.

5. Bart D. Ehrman, *The Orthodox Corruption of Scripture: The Effect of Early Christological Controversies on the Text of the New Testament* (New York: Oxford University Press, 2011) demonstrates such theological tampering, though not so broad in scope, in the New Testament.

6. Mark C. Goodacre, "Fatigue in the Synoptics." *New Testament Studies.* Vol. 44 (1998), pp. 45–58; Wheless, *Is It God's Word?*, p. 203.

Besides Elohim, there is another prominent Hebrew/biblical name for the deity, namely Yahweh (also rendered "Jehovah"). It appears that originally the names Elohim and Yahweh denoted two gods who were father and son. El Elyon, "God Most High," was the head of the Israelite pantheon, while Yahweh, one of the seventy "sons of God," was the patron god of Israel, just as Rimmon was the patron deity of Aram (Syria) and Chemosh that of Moab. At the beginning of the human race, the highest god divided his creatures into as many nations as he had sons, so that each divine prince would have a fiefdom to rule and a population to worship him.

> When Elyon gave to the nations their inheritance,
>   when he separated the sons of men,
> he fixed the bounds of the peoples
>   according to the number of the sons of El.
> For Yahweh's portion is his people,
> Jacob his allotted heritage. (Deut. 32:8–9)

But eventually the Jewish elders decided to move toward monotheism. To this end they fused El Elyon with Yahweh as well as making the other divine sons into mere "angels" ("messengers"). Soon, as part of the same package, they decided these beings were evil, which is why the nations (which they still ruled) were so wicked. They did this by reinterpreting an old myth about the sons of God mating with mortal women to produce a crop of demigods (Gen. 6:1–4), exactly as in the Greek myths of Hercules, Theseus, Perseus, etc. But this did not fit the newer understanding of monotheism, so this interbreeding suddenly became a dreadful blasphemy against nature (as in Jude verses 6–7). Sooner or later, Jews believed, Yahweh would "fire" these wicked subordinates, imprisoning them in subterranean caverns, and he would assume direct (and righteous) rule himself:

Elohim has taken his place in the divine council;
in the midst of the gods he holds judgment:
"How long will you judge unjustly
and show partiality to the wicked?
Give justice to the weak and the fatherless;
maintain the right of the afflicted and the destitute.
Rescue the weak and the needy;
deliver them from the hand of the wicked."
They have neither knowledge nor understanding,
they walk about in darkness;
all the foundations of the earth are shaken.
I say, "You are gods,
sons of Elyon, all of you;
nevertheless, you shall die like men,
and fall like any [mortal] prince."
Arise, O Elohim, judge the earth;
for to thee belong all the nations! (Psalm 82)

Was the Hebrew God Unique?

With the unearthing in 1928 of the Ras Shamra texts, Cunieform writings in the Ugaritic tongue, scholars learned much about the ancient Canaanites, their language, and their religion. For one thing, it became clear that Ugaritic (so-called from the location of the texts, Ugarit AKA Ras Shamra) was closely cognate with ancient Hebrew, so much so that, in light of it, it became clearer what certain Old Testament passages really meant. Just as significant, we realized how closely parallel the Canaanite theology was to that of ancient Israel. The chief deity bore the all-too-familiar name of El. Baal was his mighty son who had defeated the sea dragon Lotan just as Yahweh, Elyon's son, had vanquished Leviathan (both being mythic personifications of the river Litani). We read of Yahweh's victory in Psalm 74:14; 89:10; Isaiah 27:1; 51:9; Job 26:12; chapter 41. Baal was even sometimes called "Yah."[7]

After defeating the dragon, Yahweh had taken the throne beside Elyon as co-regent (Dan. 7:9–10, 13–14):

> thrones were placed
>> and one that was ancient of days took his seat;
> his raiment was white as snow,
>> and the hair of his head like pure wool;
> his throne was fiery flames,
>> its wheels were burning fire.
> A stream of fire issued
>> and came forth from before him;
> a thousand thousands served him,
>> and ten thousand times ten thousand stood before him;
> the court sat in judgment,
>> and the books were opened.
>> and behold, with the clouds of heaven
>> there came one like a son of man,
> and he came to the Ancient of Days
>> and was presented before him.
> And to him was given dominion
>> and glory and kingship,
> that all peoples, nations, and languages
>> should serve him;
> his dominion is an everlasting dominion,
>> which shall not pass away,
> and his kingdom one
>> that shall not be destroyed.

It proved to be but a natural step from making Yahweh co-regent with Elyon to identifying the two. This was probably the beginning of

---

7. Giovanni Garbini, *History and Ideology in Ancient Israel*. Trans. John Bowden (New York: Crossroad, 1988), Chapter 4, "The Origin and Development of Yahwism," pp. 52–65.

the Jewish distaste for what they deemed the "Two Powers in Heaven" heresy that threatened monotheism by placing Enoch, Yahoel, David, Moses or others at God's right hand.[8] Well, the same thing must have happened next door among the Canaanites because we start seeing references to "Aleyan Baal," or "Lord Most High" in the Ugaritic texts. Baal was accorded the same promotion via unification.

If I may say so, this is one of those cases where the evolved concept or doctrine is debunked by revealing the history of its evolution, as in Nietzsche's *Genealogy of Morals*. From there on in, you can't help seeing the human fingerprints, the tracks in the no longer virgin snow. We will, rest assured, see more instances.

Mistaken Identity?

Are these issues mere relics? Or is there any importance here for moderns? I should say there is indeed, for something like the same issues have resurfaced in our time with the resurgence of Islam. Some, nursing a grudge against the religion of Muhammad (admittedly for understandable reasons), seem to want to repudiate any possible historical kinship between Christianity and Islam, denying that the two faiths share devotion to the same God. Whatever objections one may have to Islam or Muslims, that particular claim is completely baseless. "Allah" (a contraction of "al-Illah") just means "the God." Arabic is cognate with Hebrew, just like Ugaritic, and Illah is simply a variant from the same root, "El." Yes, as we have seen, "Elohim" can be generic, not inherently referring to a particular deity, but one need not read long in the Koran to recognize plentiful names and stories from both Old and New Testaments.[9] Even if, as a

---

8. Alan F. Segal, *Two Powers in Heaven: Early Rabbinic Reports about Christianity and Gnosticism.* Studies in Judaism in Late Antiquity. Vol. 25 (Leiden: E.J. Brill, 1977); Peter Schäfer, *Two Gods in Heaven: Jewish Concepts of God in Antiquity.* Trans. Allison Brown (Princeton: Princeton University Press, 2020).

9. Abraham I. Katsch, *Judaism in the Koran:* (Perpetua, 1962).

non-Muslim, you reject the Islamic scripture as a genuine revelation from God, you cannot deny that it is *supposed* to be the Word of the same God Jews and Christians worship.

The Character of this Character

Dan Barker[10] is quite right to lament the fear-mongering scare-story nature of several biblical tales in which God plays the role of boogeyman to keep childlike believers in line. He is just as correct to highlight the absurdity of the Absolute Spirit, the Infinite Deity, the Eternal Being-itself, insisting on minor decorative details for the Tabernacle. And Barker just cannot let it rest when it comes to God's confessed "jealousy." But this is where I begin to suspect something is out of focus. Barker psychoanalyzes this paranoid, green-eyed god as harboring sexual insecurities, and I have to infer he means this deity is a psychological projection of the insecure, chauvinistic macho-men who invented him. But it seems to me that "God" is not so much a literary character as a bottling up of echoes made by the endless ventriloquism of Israelite priestcraft.

The "jealousy" of Jehovah/Yahweh is simply a function of the zeal of priestly propaganda aimed at getting the people of Israel to stop dividing their devotion (and their sacrifices, which fed the priests) between Jehovah and his competitors including Baal and Asherah. As L. Sprague de Camp shrewdly pointed out in his wonderful historical novel *The Dragon of the Ishtar Gate*, it was a question of cornering the market, as much monopolism as monotheism. But when not cynical, the prophetic threats against those who worshipped other gods were (superstitious) attempts to prevent national disaster. And this is a sub-set of the belief in divine judgment as a variety of *theodicy*: the desperate attempt to maintain a belief in divine justice in the face of crushing evidence to the contrary. It was of a piece with

---

10. Dan Barker, *God: The Most Unpleasant Character in All Fiction*. (Sterling, 2016).

the belief that epilepsy, otherwise inexplicable at the time, was the result of demon-possession.

Similarly, the ridiculous idea of God as the pickiest of interior decorators is the result of the ancient priesthood ramroding their preferences through and silencing other opinions. "God" was a ventriloquist dummy. To complain about "God" as a character is almost to fall for the scam. Look for the man, or men, *behind* the curtain.

Why on earth would God be even more neurotic than me (I don't eat vegetables) in his food choices for himself (in sacrificial offerings) and for others (via kosher laws)? You have to approach these things with an ear open to anthropology. As Mary Douglas explained,[11] most of the dietary laws, sexual behavior rules, and even taxonomical categories are typical of the systems of mores to be found in all cultures. The biblical ones strike non-Jews as odd simply because they are alien to us. We think it strange that, in some cultures people eat roaches, but we pay big bucks to dine on lobsters, which are pretty much the same thing. And in all traditional societies, there is a "sacred canopy"[12] of values, mores, customs, and laws, with religion/mythology serving as the capstone. Things are *as* they are because Zeus, Brahma, or Jehovah ordained them that way. So who are you, pipsqueak, to say different? As Durkheim said, society *is* religion.[13] Or at least it *used* to be. It is the pre-scientific way in which ancients and primitives expressed the ultimate importance and inviolability of their social systems. God and the gods were simply figureheads, totems.

---

11. Mary Douglas, *Purity and Danger: An Analysis of Concepts of Pollution and Taboo* (Baltimore: Penguin Books, 1966), chapter 3, "The Abominations of Leviticus," pp. 54–72.

12. Peter L. Berger, *The Sacred Canopy: Elements of a Sociological Theory of Religion* (Garden City: Doubleday Anchor Books, 1969).

13. Emile Durkheim, *The Elementary Forms of the Religious Life*. Trans. Joseph Ward Swain. A Free Press Paperback (New York: Macmillan, 1915, 1965), pp. 479–487.

Is God a Goddess?

I believe that the whole business of "inclusive language" referring to the deity is a great bit of irony. Those who think that calling God "she" somehow gives women their due are blithely contenting themselves with a crumb tossed them by the patriarchal establishment. For one thing, it is absolutely clear that the biblical "God" (Elohim, Yahweh) is a male. He had a consort, Asherah, as most of Israel always knew. Asherah reigned beside Yahweh in the Jerusalem temple for over half the years it stood.[14] She was periodically driven out, along with the rest of the Israelite pantheon, by the Cromwellian zeal of the Deuteronomic School.

All this mythology is simply the same as Canaanite religion anyway (it *is* Canaanite religion!), where it is equally clear that El is a male, Asherah is his wife, and Baal is his son, Anath being Baal's wife, etc.

Another thing: It would be anachronistic to refer to this God as "she" since he is a literary character like Zeus, a male figure. One would never make Ares or Hercules or Thor or Krishna a woman. Thus I refer to God in my discussion of the biblical stories, including the implicit narratives of Pauline and Johannine theology ("God sent forth his Son . . ."), as "he." But, on the other hand, as we will see, the God of theological apologists has little to do with the blatantly mythic deity of the Bible, anyway.

But what about our own modern endeavors to do creative theology? Should we call God "she" in this context at least? I think not. It is important to see that the very notion of a single divine monarch issuing commands is a patriarchal notion, a phallocentric doctrine. It is to exalt the one over the many ("king of the hill"), and to choose as the main image of divine influence that of coercion. The move toward monotheism, with Elohim as the only God, represented a

---

14. Raphael Patai, *The Hebrew Goddess*. A Discus Book (New York: Avon Books, 1978), pp. 38–39.

"cornering of the market" by one faction of priests, a symbolic tool to impose the totalistic rule of the human monarch through the agency of a single priesthood. All other power centers, divine or human, were driven out. Popular religion, polytheism, was crushed by the Temple elite, the dominant faction. Monotheism perpetuates this, as does the doctrine that there can be only one true religion.

Thus for us to call the biblical/Christian God "she" (or to call Jesus the "Child" of God) to try to eliminate gender bias is grossly premature. It leaves in place the patriarchalist presupposition of monarchial monotheism. We still have the vertical rule of a transcendent monarch over the servile many. We still have essentially male rule over the system of belief. The cosmetic change of a couple of words does not change that.

Indeed, it is quite clear that ancient Israel was not monotheistic in its theology, despite the monotheistic convictions of the final editors of the canon. I doubt that earliest Christianity was monotheistic either. The emergence of the doctrine of the Trinity (as we will see) is perhaps best viewed as a late attempt to make Christianity monotheistic after the fact, just as Hindu Trinitarianism sought to forge three distinct deities (Brahama, Vishnu, Siva) into one.

So is the biblical Jehovah the God of present-day Theism? Jaco Gericke[15] has argued quite effectively that, when modern theists think they are defending the God of the Bible they are actually engaging in defending a highly abstract philosophical God-concept. They mean to vindicate "the God of Abraham, Isaac and Jacob" while they are actually defending the "God of the Philosophers." And there is an impassable gulf between the two. Even attempting to speak of God in philosophical terms introduces a huge problem. The biblical deity is *personal*, like Zeus. The philosophically defined deity is *abstract*. To pursue theological speech philosophically makes the whole biblical depiction of God highly problematical. And yet we

---

15. Jaco Gericke, *What is a God?: Philosophical Perspectives on Divine Essence in the Hebrew Bible* (Edinburgh: T&T Clark, 2018).

cannot seem to avoid taking that "wrong" turn since, as Paul Tillich[16] says, biblical statements inevitably raise ontological (philosophical) questions that they do not answer but which they implicitly invite us to answer. For instance, when Isaiah's God proclaims, "As far as the sky is above the earth, so far do my thoughts transcend your thoughts," we have to ask how we can even begin to stammer about the likeness of this God. This realization is nothing new. Already the eleventh-century theologian Anselm of Canterbury admitted that, being changelessly immutable, God cannot be said even to love us! Theology is reduced to saying there is *something* in the divine nature that corresponds to our notion of love and merits the term in some derivative sense.

Thomas Aquinas, two centuries later, tried to deal with the problem of, as twentieth- century theologians would call it, "God-language" by delineating three different types of speech: *Univocal* speech would be a direct, one-to-one reference, describing something in exactly the terms we are using, literally true. But this is of no help speaking of God for obvious reasons. Second, we may use *equivocal* speech, where the same word refers to two totally different realities. An example of such attempted theological speech is when some say that it would be wrong if you knew what Hitler was going to do and did not kill him when you had the chance, but it is all right for God not to have squashed Adolf *because "right" doesn't mean the same thing for us and for God.* Well, then, why use the same word at all?

But third, we might speak of God by *analogy*: a term is appropriate in many ways, to many degrees, up and down a scale with God at the top, ourselves in the middle, animals nearer the bottom. Your dog is happy when you get home for the evening. Does the dog love you? Well, not like you love your spouse. But there is a continuity.

---

16. Paul Tillich, *Biblical Religion and the Search for Ultimate Reality*. James W. Richards Lecture in the Christian Religion, University of Virginia 1951–52 (Chicago: University of Chicago Press, 1955), p. 83.

Dogs are pack animals and feel great security when the whole pack is together in their den for the night. This emotion lacks the tenderness and complexity of human love, whether of spouse or family, but *it is the same **sort** of thing*. Does God love you in the same way you love a spouse, a child, a parent? No, but whatever it is that is true of God in his covenant commitment is as analogous to human love as human love is to a dog's "love," only in the reverse direction, higher.

Eastern Orthodox theologians have a different approach, the *Via Negativa*. (This is also called Apophatic Theology.) There is a quicker realization here, it seems to me, that human speech about God, even what Aquinas supposes we might be able to say by way of analogy, will fall so far short of saying anything intelligible about God that we might as well just stop gabbing and get lost in awe and worship. This approach is less rationalistic, more mystical. We can hardly avoid idolatry if we think we are actually describing God, because a concept of God your mind could grasp would *ipso facto* be smaller than the mind grasping it! But if we just concentrate on disabusing ourselves of false notions, *mis*conceptions of God, then at least we will be closer to the truth about God than when we were led astray by erroneous, superstitious views about him. You may not be getting warm, but at least you're getting less cold![17] In fact, notice how many of the "attributes" of God that follow *sound* like positive statements about God but are really *negations of limitations* which we understand better. I know what it means to be stuck in one place at a time; I have no idea what it would be like to be omnipresent: it is just the negation of being stuck in one place at a time. With this caveat in mind, let's review the traditional attributes of God.

First, *eternity*: God exists outside of time and does not experience a succession of moments, since the latter is a matter of the limitation of human consciousness. C.S. Lewis explains:

---

17. A great discussion of this approach is Vladimir Lossky, *The Mystical Theology of the Eastern Church* (Crestwood, NY: St. Vladimir's Press, 1976).

But suppose God is outside and above the Time-line. In that case, what we call "tomorrow" is visible to Him in just the same way as what we call "today." All the days are "Now" for Him. He does not remember you doing things yesterday; He simply sees you doing them, because, though you have lost yesterday, He has not. He does not "foresee" you doing things tomorrow; He simply sees you doing them; because, though tomorrow is not yet there for you, it is for Him.[18]

Biblical references (Deut. 33:27; Ps. 90; Isa. 57:15; 1 Tim. 1:17; 6:5–16) to God's eternal existence may intend that God does experience duration but has always done so and always will. The "timelessness" interpretation appears at least as early as St. Augustine and represents Platonist interpretation. If God is outside the time continuum, what does this imply for God *acting*? Does he only *appear* to act? Is that merely a case of anthropomorphism?

Second, *omniscience*: God is all-knowing. If God is aware of everything at once, we may ask if he experiences linear thinking. He certainly need not pursue a train of thought out to completion. He must already know the answer—and all answers! Buddhism imagined the Buddha to be only, as Freud might say, *pre-consciously* omniscient.[19] All knowledge was *available* to him whenever he required it, as the ray projected by his third eye could scan the universe in a single moment. That is a way of making something like omniscience compatible with individual consciousness. Otherwise, we may be bound to think of the omniscient God as pure consciousness rather than as a conscious individual. The Upanishads speak of Brahman (the ultimate Godhead) as *Satchitananda*, or "Being-Consciousness-Bliss." Or we might adopt Aristotle's notion of God as "Thought thinking itself." Only then we may have to reckon with

---

18. Lewis, *Mere Christianity*, pp. 148–149.

19. Edward J. Thomas, *The Life of Buddha as Legend and History*. The History of Civilization (London: Routledge & Kegan Paul, 1949), p. 213.

the possibility that, as pure thought, God is not conscious of any-thing else but himself, being lost in pure contemplation!

Third, *omnipotence*: In the Bible God's omnipotence seems to mean "no more than" that no one can gainsay his plans; he is the most powerful. This is not quite the same question as whether he is technically "all-powerful." If he is the latter, then should we picture God as "the power of being," by which all things including Satan and the AIDS virus are upheld? Martin Luther and Paul Tillich thought so. Or is he an indefatigable controller, a man at a switchboard, con-trolling everything, the cause of everything that happens? John Cal-vin seems to have thought so. Or is God *potentially* controlling but *actually* self-limiting, allowing other wills to prevail in the short run for the sake of freedom? Arminians think so. But would this last op-tion be compatible with divine Providence, the notion that God is at work knitting all events into a grand tapestry? Calvinists claim that a limitation of God's actual, hands-on exercise of authority must logi-cally lead straight to the "who's-minding-the-store?" creed of Deism.

We are given to think that God can do all that can be *done*, but not necessarily all that can be *said*. Why? Because some "deeds" to which we challenge God are gibberish with no coherent content: "Can God draw a square circle?" A *what*? He can't draw a four-sided triangle, either, because both are just a mish-mash of words, not an imaginable notion. Nor can he create a rock too heavy for himself to lift, a river too wide for him to cross. Such "chores" boil down to ask-ing, "Can God be omnipotent and *not* omnipotent at the same time and in the same sense?"

Does Omnipotence imply predestination? A good question, which is why we will also deal with predestination elsewhere in this book.

Fourth, *immutability*: God does not change (Jas. 1:17; Mal. 3:6). But, again, then we must ask if an immutable God can act at all, since acting is changing. The minute God creates, has he not changed from being a *potential* creator to being an *actual* creator? The biblical writers seem to mean only that God is *reliable*, that his *character* does not change, which would still leave him free to act. Modern Process theologians, influenced by Alfred North Whitehead and his unintelligible books, suggest that God has two natures, a *Primordial* nature which does *not* change and which accounts for his moral integrity, and a *Consequent* nature, which *does* change, acting and reacting as it takes account of the changing world. How can an immutable God even keep tabs on the world? In this manner Process theologians seek to return (sort of) to "biblical personalism." But have they? Isn't it obvious that they are, first, just making it up as they go along? And second, that they have only traded one abstraction for another? Theirs is no Jehovah, even if that's nothing to bemoan.

Fifth, *omnipresence*: God is everywhere present, not that he is distributed in space, there being more of him in a pint bottle than a gallon jug, as St. Augustine pointed out, but rather he transcends space as he does time. Thus wherever we are, God is *present to* us, "not in the spaces we know but between them."[20] He does not move to keep up with us. Nor is he an atmosphere extended around us. Relevant texts include Jeremiah 23:23–24 (which, however, does seem to think of God spatially extended); Psalm 139; 1 Kings 8:27; and Acts 17:27.

Sixth, *aseity*: God is self-sufficient and invulnerable to harm or to influence. In the Bible we see this emphasis in statements that God cannot be hungry, requiring the ministrations of mortals, as if he were a zoo animal (Acts 17:25), and that he is incapable of being cheated. But the larger implications are great. As Hosea Ballou[21] noted, we cannot imagine that God requires of human beings an

---

20. H.P. Lovecraft, "The Dunwich Horror."

21. Hosea Ballou, *A Treatise on Atonement; in Which the Finite Nature of Sin is Argued, its Cause and Consequences as Such; the Necessity and Nature of Atonement; and its Glorious Consequences in the Final Reconciliation of All Men to Holiness and Happiness* (Hallowell: C. Spaulding, 3rd ed., 1828), pp. 72–73.

atonement to make good the injury humans have done to his sacred honor—as if God can be harmed by puny humans! Can he even be displeased by sin?

Seventh, *simplicity*: God is not a composite entity but instead must be, in Derrida's terms, Originary Presence. There cannot have been some process by which God "got the way he is."

Eighth, *holiness*: Originally, as Rudolf Otto[22] shows, the notion of the holiness of God did not at first connote moral righteousness. No, the divine was understood/experienced as being above and beyond worldly distinctions such as good and evil. The holiness of the divine was rather the *Wholly-Otherness* of God, an uncanny and overpowering sense of alien presence. One senses that the Holy is majestic, august, that it is full of awe, full of being and power, so that one is as nothing compared with it. Wherefore the mortal cringes, not in moral guilt, but in ontological shame: "I am nothing!" The Holy catalyzes the Numinous experience, an experience of holy terror or panic on the one hand, but of irresistible fascination on the other. In the same moment, the same fact of the Holy's absolute *otherness* both repels us out of fear because of our inadequacy and attracts us out of the sense that it has, or *is*, precisely what we require for a fulfillment nothing in this world can give.

By placing God outside and above the time stream so that he sees all moments simultaneously, one makes him "the God above God,"[23] no longer a willing, acting person but rather "Brahman without qualities." By contrast, time-contained creatures "exist" in a realm of illusion (maya, Samsara), and this renders our much-vaunted "free will" illusory, a trick of the light. Human action is thus exactly like the "events" and "decisions" in a novel. It is all present in the book before

22. Rudolf Otto, *The Idea of the Holy: An Inquiry into the Non-Rational Factor in the Idea of the Divine and its Relation to the Rational*. Trans. John H. Harvey (London: Oxford University Press, 1924),

23. Paul Tillich, *Systematic Theology, Vol. II, Existence and the Christ* (Chicago: University of Chicago Press, 1957), p. 12.

we open it and start reading. It *seems* to be happening, characters making decisions, choosing actions—but only in the eyes of the reader as he moves through the text. This is the final irony: philosophical Christian theology must logically reveal itself as (Hindu) non-dualism. We have imagined, ala Philippians 2:6–11, that the divine Son "emptied himself" of his divine attributes to walk the earth as a mortal man. But must we not say equally that the extra-temporal Godhead, the "God above the God of Theism"[24] "emptied himself," too, into the spatio-temporal field of finitude—in order to create, to avenge, to speak and act and redeem. In short, he must become the Demiurge of Gnosticism, the Isvara of Vedanta Hinduism,[25] the Adi-Buddha of the Mahayana. This is what it has to mean if "God is both a person and the negation of himself as a person."[26]

Speaking of novels, it seems to me that the damning flaw in the predestination concept reveals itself when we compare the predestined life to a novel or a film script. The characters in the story think they are making their own decisions, nor do they suspect they are puppets whose strings are being pulled by a being who exists beyond their narrative world. In the same way, if the doctrine of predestination were true, *no one would know about it.* All the Calvinists worrying whether they are truly among the elect are like a fictional character who wonders what the author has in store for him tomorrow. That doesn't happen in novels. It would be a violation of the narrative time-line. It is like a time-travel story in which the hero knows what is scheduled to happen in his future; can he contrive to avoid it? What a mess.

---

24. Paul Tillich, *The Courage to Be* (New Haven: Yale University Press, 1952), p. 187.

25. Raymond Panikkar, *The Unknown Christ of Hinduism* (London: Darton, Longman & Todd), 1964), pp. 126–127.

26. Tillich, *Biblical Religion and the Search for Ultimate Reality*, p. 85.

2

Winging It

The Secret History of Angels

Angels seem to be all the rage these days. From a previous near-invisibility, they seem to be everywhere you look. What? Price, are you mad? Are you seeing things? Yes, I am. Don't worry, I'm not seeing real angels, mind you, no glowing entities with wings. I'm just seeing them on calendars and T-shirts and coffee mugs and, of course, on network TV schlockumentaries where every paranormal fad has its day. Like the TV evangelists, the network programmers allow the Nielsen ratings to govern their theology. If enough people will watch, then it must be true.

So one can hardly escape from angels, at least at the moment. They are having, as we poor mortals do, their fifteen minutes of fame. It seems to me you can divide the current interest in angels into two categories. On the one hand, angels have become a kind of variation on the theme of UFO contactees. People are writing books about their "close encounters" of the angelic kind. It's more of the general New Age fixation on supposedly higher beings who can give us a helping hand.

To be honest, before tarring angels with the brush of Shirley MacLaine and Ramtha, I ought to tell you that Schleiermacher and

28

other Liberal theologians also compared angels to beings from other planets. Maybe it's not so crazy an idea. We'll explore that more below.

This kind of thing has happened in many cultures before. It is a sign of a religious crisis. As Gabriel Vahanian[27] would say, the fad belief in angels is just the contrary of what it might at first seem. It might seem a sign of religious renewal, but instead, like belief in Occultism, it is a sign of the Death of God. It is an exotic last gasp of religion in a jaded society. A retreat into superstition.

And it's happened before. In ancient Judaism, people lost sight of the One God and turned to angel worship. In West Africa and in pre-Islamic Arabia people began to believe that a great High God had retreated and left us to deal with a celestial bureaucracy.

On the other hand, today's rage of angels may be no more than the cat fad: you know, all the Kliban posters and mugs? Angels have been reduced to mascots, pets, essentially no more than Valentine cherubs. So some people take them way too seriously, others not seriously enough.

Not seriously enough? Am I telling you I believe in angels? No, not really. But I believe there is an important truth here, and one perhaps neglected in the current time when angels are all the rage. To tell you what this is, I need to go back and fill in some of the background of the angel myth.

Angels of Our Nature

The historical development of angelology, whether in ancient myth or modern entertainment, is a fascinating story that remains unsuspected by all but scholars. I want to present the high points of that history, connecting the dots in an accessible manner.

Angelology seems to have been borrowed (with much else) from

27. Gabriel Vahanian, *The Death of God: The Culture of our Post-Christian Era* (New York: George Braziller, 1961).

Zoroastrianism by Jewish theologians during or after the Babylonian Exile, once the Persians (Zoroastrian in faith) took over the Babylonian Empire. The Persians resettled Jewish colonists back home in the Holy Land and financed the rebuilding of the Temple and the reestablishment of Judaism. It seems likely that the version of Judaism imposed by Ezra, a Jewish scribe working for the Persian state, was essentially a variety of Zoroastrianism, introducing doctrines including an evil Satan, an apocalyptic view of history, and a virgin-born messiah who would raise the dead for the Final Judgment. Jews who accepted this form of Judaism were called Pharisees ("Parsees," i.e., Zoroastrians). *Angelology entered Judaism at this point.*

Angels are a combination of two Zoroastrian notions: *Frahvashis* were the spirit doubles of all individuals. They had existed in heaven and became incarnate only when Ahura Mazda (=God) summoned them to aid him in battle against Ahriman (= the Anti-God). With this notion Zoroastrians combined something like the Norse Valkyries, warrior maidens who roamed the battlefield, harvesting the souls of the fallen heroes for heavenly glory. The result of the fusion was a large group of heavenly watchers who supervised the righteous but also somehow were the *higher selves of the righteous.* This, the original meaning of angels, has great spiritual significance, as opposed to mere mythology.

This is the way we are to understand Matthew's reference to individuals and their personal angels. "Make sure that you do not cause one of these little ones to stumble, for their angels always behold the face of my Father in heaven." Luke has the same idea in the Book of Acts, when Peter is on death row and is miraculously rescued. But then he makes his way to the house where his friends are praying for his release. And in one of the funniest moments of the Bible, he is knocking at the door, the maid sees him and is so flabbergasted that she leaves him waiting outside while she runs in to tell the others - *and they don't believe her!* Some faith! They figure it's too late. Peter must already be dead. Who's at the door, then? "It must be his angel." Interesting! It tells us they thought your guardian angel must look just like you. It even implies that your guardian angel was your ghost! Your soul. And that is our clue.

According to the esoteric doctrines of suppressed Christian sects, your guardian angel was indeed your higher self. It was part of the doctrine that you have various physical and psychic layers, seven levels of *you*. The grossest was the physical body, while the most refined was the spirit. And the goal of salvation was to free the spirit from its incarceration in the flesh. This is why the Corinthian Gnostics scoffed at the doctrine of the resurrection of the flesh.

How would you disengage the spirit Self from the fleshly self? By meditation and study. And then at death the spirit could soar free and return to its primordial unity with the Divine Pleroma. It's all very much like Yoga.

There were special sacraments to help out. One was called the Bridal Chamber. It is mentioned in the Gospel of Philip and the Gospel of Thomas. In it one prepared oneself for a vision in which one beheld Christ as the bridegroom of the soul. Another image for the same thing was that you would behold your own spiritual twin, your guardian angel, your higher self, and this, too, was Christ.

Here is a profound piece of spirituality: that if you are, as evangelists often say, to meet Christ, it will be meeting your true self for the first time. An old Zen saying puts it this way: "If you meet the Buddha on the road—kill him!" Because the only true Buddha there can be is the one hidden inside you, waiting to come out.

Earth Angels and Superstars

Were there no angels in the Old Testament before Zoroastrianism rubbed off on it? It all depends on what one means by "angels." *Cherubim* were common Near Eastern myth-creatures, probably personified storm clouds and etymologically related to European Griffins (gryphons). They were pictured as strange chimeras, sometimes as winged bulls with human faces (as in Assyria), winged lions with human faces, or just winged men and women. In the Old Testament they are assigned the duty of guarding God's treasures from the sticky fingers of greedy mortals. Hence Genesis chapter 3 has Jehovah post a Cherub at the Tree of Life to keep Adam and his descendants away from it. Seth and Eve seek a piece of the fruit for Adam when he is on his deathbed, but the Cherub will not relent.[28] Cherubs also guard God's signet ring in Eden and the Ark of the Covenant in the Temple. Giant Cherub statues cover the box with their sculpted and gold-plated wings. The lid of the Ark features two humanoid Cherubs. (The Talmud tells us they were male and female and locked in sexual intercourse!) These are the celestial entities Ezekiel beholds upholding the divine throne chariot in Ezekiel 1–2. John sees them in Revelation 5, too.

The Bible also mentions *Seraphim*, "fiery ones." Judging by their iconic depictions in Egypt and elsewhere, Seraphim appear to have been blazing serpents with wings (like Quetzalcoatl) and with human hands or feet if their assigned tasks required them. Their major biblical appearance is in Isaiah chapter 6, where each one has six wings that cover either their own faces or Adonai's, presumably because any of their countenances are too fearsome for mortals to behold.

The trouble is, neither Cherubs nor Seraphs are ever called "angels," which is simply the Hebrew word for "messengers." It is the same in the Greek language of the New Testament. Thus when the text refers to "angels," it is not always easy to tell what is meant. Sometimes, as in the Sodom and Gomorrah story (Gen. 19), all we are told is that God brought a couple of "messengers" to send on a fact-finding tour of the Dead Sea Valley where Sodom was located. They are seen by the locals and naturally taken for mortal strangers. They do not sport haloes or wings. In fact, *the Bible never describes angels in this way.*

---

28. Esther Casier Quinn, *The Quest of Seth for the Oil of Life* (Chicago: University of Chicago Press, 1962).

By the way, it suddenly makes sense when we read of the rationalistic Sadducee sect in the gospels that, though fierce partisans of traditional scripture, they did not believe in angels. How could they *not*? Well, it wasn't so clear to them, perhaps, that the Hebrew Bible ever mentioned "angels" as we, or their Jewish contemporaries, pictured them.

All those mentions of *"the angel of the Lord," "the angel of God,"* etc., certainly involved a heavenly being coming to earth to visit mortals, right? Weren't they angels in our sense? No, they are appearances of God himself, as when Zeus took human form in the Greek myths. Hence theologians call these appearances "theophanies," manifestations of God in person. And thus they function to safeguard God's transcendence. Surely he could not stoop to dirty his hands in such matters as molding Adam from mud or carving the words into the stone slabs of the Ten Commandments, or playing hide-and-seek with Moses in a bush. In all such cases it was instead the angel of the Lord.

Who were the mysterious *"sons of God"* mentioned here and there in the Old Testament? Numerous references make it clear that Israelite religion was originally polytheistic, just like the surrounding Canaanite cultures. It was only much later that history began to be retold as if originally monotheistic Israelites had borrowed other gods from neighboring cultures. No, monotheism was a late growth, appearing for the first time in Jeremiah, writing directly before the Exile began, and the Second Isaiah, writing just before it was over, some half-century later. In retrospect, the editors of scripture rewrote or reinterpreted the mentions of sons of god and lesser Israelite gods as references to angels, heavenly flunkies of a single deity.

The Seven Archangels (the names vary, but are generally Michael, Gabriel, Raphael, Uriel, Rakiel, Jeremiel, and Zauriel) seem to be a direct survival of the seven Archangels of Ahura Mazda (Vohu Mana, etc.), each embodying one of his chief attributes. What do we know of each Archangel from ancient lore?

Gabriel was God's herald, the biblical version of Hermes/Mercury: he delivers messages to Daniel, to the Virgin Mary (in both Luke and the Koran), and to the Prophet Muhammad. Apparently it is he who is to blow the trumpet signaling the Final Judgment. *Michael* ("Who is like God?") leads the heavenly forces against the Dragon in the War in Heaven. He represents Israel before God's throne as an advocate and protector in Daniel (10:13) striving against the protective angels (originally national gods) of other kingdoms. *Raphael* is the angel of healing, featured in the Book of Tobit. *Uriel* (Oriel) serves as the angel of revelation. Presumably his name is related to that of the oracular dice, the Urim and Thummim. He appears as the interpreting angel during apocalyptic visions/journeys. Uriel stars in 2 Esdras. *Zauriel* (or Azrael) was the Angel of Death, the Grim Reaper.

The Seven Archangels also represent the known planets in biblical times. As such they have been mythologized into God's "eyes" (from the Persian spy system, "eyes of the king"), constantly scrutinizing the earth.[29] The 24 elders in Revelation 4 are the Decans, and there are many other astrological features permeating that book.[30]

Matthew features Zoroastrian astrologers ("magi" from Parthia) coming to honor the young king, having seen his star. Yet once they arrive, a moving star locates the specific house, something no horoscope is going to do! A moving star? Even in ancient biblical cosmology this makes no sense—unless stars were equated with angels.

"Elemental spirits" (mentioned in Galatians) were angels in charge of the various celestial treasuries of snow, rain, etc., and their release. They were also known in Stoicism. They become the Gnostic Archons. Paul makes them the promulgators, if not even the authors, of the Torah (Gal. 3:8–10, 19–20). They are hard to distinguish in

---

29. Margaret Barker, *The Gate of Heaven: The History and Symbolism of the Temple in Jerusalem* (London: S.P.C.K., 1991), p. 29.

30. Bruce J. Malina, *On the Genre and Message of Revelation: Star Visions and Sky Journeys* (Peabody: Hendrickson Publishers, 1995).

New Testament thought from the "Principalities and Powers" (Rom. 8:38; Col. 1:16; 2:15), earlier referred to as the fallen Sons of God, still (corruptly) ruling behind the thrones of the nations.

Angels Remythologized

The cosmology of the New Testament is essentially mythical in character. The world is viewed as a three-storied structure, with the earth in the center, the heaven above, and the underworld beneath. Heaven is the abode of God and of the celestial beings—the angels. . . . [The earth] is the scene of the supernatural activity of God and his angels on the one hand, and of Satan and his demons on the other. These supernatural forces intervene in the course of nature and in all that men think and do.

Now that the forces and the laws of nature have been discovered, we can no longer believe in spirits, whether good or evil.

If the truth of the New Testament proclamation is to be preserved, the only way is to demythologize it.

These quotes from Rudolf Bultmann's famous essay "New Testament and Mythology" provide us with a paradigm for discussing the Liberal Protestant theological outlook on angelology. First of all, like Bultmann, many Liberal theologians regard the angels of the Old and New Testaments as survivals of the archaic mythology of the Babylonians and Persians. Their appearance as heralds and messengers of God seems to presuppose a literally spatial picture of God and the world. God's transcendence is mythically portrayed as a great distance which must be bridged by characters like Hermes, the messenger from Mount Olympus. As such, Liberals suggest, angels may be retained only as poetic language in the modern world. Yet Liberals do not pretend to know what can and cannot exist in the universe. They grant that superhuman beings like the biblical angels at least theoretically might exist:

More than ever nowadays, as we learn more and more of the inconceivable vastness of space and time and of the infinite proliferation of worlds, it becomes a probability of the highest order that there are or have been or will be beings that surpass man in the hierarchy of beings. (John Macquarrie)[31]

It seems probable that some created superhuman persons, formerly human beings of earth [i.e., glorified saints], and perhaps others too [e.g., extraterrestrials] do exist. Some such beings may have responsibilities which affect us for weal or woe as the scriptures teach. (L. Harold deWolf)[32]

[The] conception [of angels] contains in itself nothing impossible and does not conflict with the basis of the religious consciousness in general. (Friedrich Schleiermacher)[33]

Yet it should be remembered that these theologians are not looking for a reason to believe in angels. They are not trying to vindicate the accuracy of Bible tales in which angelic beings appear. Rather, they are just trying to be open to all possibilities: beings analogous to the biblical angels might well exist, not that this proves they do! In any case, belief in them is not seen as a requirement for true Christian faith. Take them or leave them.

But even if such beings exist, such a curiosity would not really be the theologically relevant point about angels. Here we arrive at the second half of the agenda proposed by Bultmann, i.e., demythologizing (or interpreting) the myth after it has been identified as such. John Macquarrie[34] expresses this concern:

---

31. John Macquarrie, *Principles of Christian Theology* (New York: Scribners, 1966), p. 215.

32. L. Harold deWolf, *A Theology for the Living Church* (New York: Harper & Row, 1960), p. 129.

33. Friedrich Schleiermacher, *The Christian Faith.* Trans. D.M. Baillie, W.R. Matthews, Edith Sandbach-Marshall, A.B. Macaulay, Alexander Grieve, J.Y. Campbell, R.W. Stewart, and H.R. Mackintosh (Edinburgh: T. & T. Clark, 1928), p. 156.

34. Macquarrie, *Principles of Christian Theology*, pp. 216, 217.

Apart altogether from the question of whether such purely spiritual creatures may exist, there is theological significance in this idea of the angelic. . . . Negatively, the concept of angelic being sets a boundary to aspirations of human existence.

Angelic (pure spiritual) existence is expressly differentiated from human existence, so as to warn us against hyper-spiritual *hubris*. We are flesh and blood and must not fall into the spiritual pride known historically as "angelism" as when one feels invulnerable to sin or above all human contact. Indeed, as the myth of the fallen angels tells us, spiritual sins are the worst of all. The importance of "angels" here is to show us what we are *not*.

Dutch theologian Hendrikus Berkhof[35] undertakes a full-scale interpretation of Paul's doctrine of the Dominions, Thrones, Principalities, and Powers. The titles have survived in classical Christian angelology, but they have come to refer to benign angels, whereas for Paul they are much more ambiguous, and usually evil. Berkhof shows that Paul had already begun a demythologizing process and tended to think of these "powers" (*exousia*) and "elemental spirits" (*stoicheia*) as personifications of the various "orders of creation" which uphold, organize, and govern human existence. Various Pauline texts (e.g., Rom. 8:38f; 1 Cor. 2:8; 15:24–26; Gal. 4:1–5; Eph. 1:20f; 2:1f; 3:10; 6:12; Col. 1:16; 2:15) suggest that Paul enumerated among these Powers human government, Jewish Law, moral and ritual codes, astrology, public opinion, religion, and philosophy, pretty much anything institutionalized. No doubt he would have considered the organized Church one of the Powers.

Paul understands such orders of creation as performing an indispensable function, created in Christ at the dawn of time for this purpose. To them God has assigned the job of school-master for the human race till maturity arrives at the coming of Christ (Gal. 4:1–

---

35. Hendrikus Berkhof, *Christ and the Powers*. Trans. John Howard Yoder (Scottdale: Herald Press, 1962).

5). But even though the powers do carry out their legitimate function as bulwarks against chaos, hindering the "war of all against all" (Thomas Hobbes; cf., 2 Thes. 2:6–8), there is nonetheless something radically wrong. The Powers, like the rest of the world, are themselves fallen and corrupt. Instead of being servants of God and human beings, they bully mankind with idolatrous claims of ultimacy. They have become "gods" (Gal. 4:8) and rebels against Christ, their rightful master. We feel completely dominated and determined by these Powers. (We can tell from this kind of talk that early Christians were sectarian dissenters from surrounding social mores and rules to whatever extent they could get away with it.)

But by his cross Christ has broken these Powers, exposing them as the illusions they are. He has "disarmed" them (Col. 2:15). Think of the expose and utter deflation of the medicine show quack in the special effects booth in Oz once Toto pulls the curtain back to reveal him. Christians will still surely face the wrath of the Powers if they defy them, but they are henceforth liberated from the fear of death that would have hitherto bound them. Identifying with Christ, they are "crucified to the world" (Gal. 6:14), having won a costly freedom which both enables and obliges them to say that Jesus, not Caesar, is Lord. Wherever the cross is proclaimed, freedom from the Powers is realized. They still perform their functions but now as the servants they were intended to be. At least Christians will pay them no more respect than that, no longer cringing at their dictates, but showing appropriate cynicism at their tall claims. Christians will take an ideology with only qualified seriousness, will put their trust completely in no this-worldly strategy, will never support a state that makes absolute claims for itself. They will not return to a dead moral legalism and will defy social convention if need be. They will not idolize Mammon. They will not love their lives unto the death. The final subjugation waits for the eschaton, but Christians participate in it, and in its freedom, already.

Whether or not one believes in literal angels, fallen or not, this

sociological demythologizing (or remythologizing?) appears re-
markably trenchant as a way of understanding our own position in
modern society, dominated by supra-personal Entities like multina-
tional corporations, monopolistic social media, ideological intimi-
dation, Political Correctness, etc.

3

Satan's Sunday School

Lewis versus Lucifer

I believe C.S. Lewis was right on target with this comment about Dualism and its relativistic, ultimately nihilistic implications:

> The two powers, or spirits, or gods—the good one or the bad one—are supposed to be quite independent. They both existed from all eternity. Neither of them made the other, neither of them has a more right than the other to call itself God. Each of them thinks it is good and thinks the other is bad. One of them likes hatred and cruelty, the other likes love and mercy. Now what do we mean when we call one of them the Good Power and the other the Bad Power? . . . [Do we mean merely] that we happen to prefer the one to the other[?][36]

Lewis was thinking of a version of ancient Zoroastrianism but would have had the same objection to Manicheanism or any other oppositional Dualism (i.e., not a complementary version like Taoism). Zoroastrianism was trying to exonerate God (Ahura Mazda) from the charge of creating evil. He didn't—someone *else* did, Ahriman,

---

36. Lewis, *Mere Christianity*, p. 48.

the evil Anti-God. Yes, this compromises the omnipotence of the deity, but it maintains his absolute righteousness. As we have seen, Pharisaic Jews (precursors of Rabbinic Judaism) adopted major elements of Persian Zoroastrianism. They saw in this doctrine of God's opposite number a valuable way to solve the problem of evil. They decided to embrace it for themselves. And to this end they recruited Satan for the role.

In the Old Testament, we meet a servant/son of God called "the Satan," not a name but a title meaning "the Adversary," combining the roles of a master of sting operations and a prosecuting attorney.[37] He tested the mettle of God's favorites, to see if they were as righteous as they were cracked up to be. Even in the New Testament he primarily performs the same function, though he is beginning to be remodeled in the likeness of Ahriman.[38] He gets conflated with Leviathan (Rev. 12:3) and Beelzebul (Mark 3:22–23), too. In Zoroastrianism, Ahriman relieved the righteous Creator Ahura Mazda of the burden of theodicy. Ahriman was the polluted fountain of evil. And now, so was Satan. It was planned that the new Persianized Satan would get Jehovah off the hook, but, logically, it failed. You see, Ahriman and Ahura Mazda were basically equal. But Satan was defined as a fallen angel, distinctly inferior to God.[39] This meant that God could still be charged with allowing Satan, once fallen, to wreak havoc in heaven and earth. Back to square one.

Could it be . . . SATAN?

The Fall of Lucifer is a late myth, compounded from various out-of-context Old Testament quotes (Gen. 3, Isa. 14, Ezek. 28). When God unveiled the newly created Adam, he commanded the angels to bow

37. Neil Forsyth, *The Old Enemy: Satan and the Combat Myth* (Princeton: Princeton University Press, 1987), p. 110.

38. Otto, *Idea of the Holy*, pp. 77 ff.

39. Lewis, *Mere Christianity*, pp. 50–51.

before him (Heb. 1:6, originally referring to Adam). Lucifer and his faction refused and decided to remove God from the throne. They lost the ensuing war (Rev. 12:7–9). Various non-canonical texts tell us that Satan was granted one tenth of his rebel angels to aid him in tempting/testing mortals. Demon possession was often ascribed to these malevolent spooks. Let's review the stages and sources of the formation of the myth.

In *Genesis 6:1–4* the Sons of God mate with mortal women and beget the Nephilim, mythical ancestors of the Anakim, a Canaanite people of great stature. (See Num. 13:28, 32–33; Deut. 3:11; 2 Sam. 21:15–22.) This story is implicitly made into the cause for the corruption that necessitated the Flood of Noah, once the compiler of Genesis sandwiches it between the introduction of Noah and the Flood story proper. But originally there was no vilification of the Sons; it was just a way of accounting for the imposing height (six and a half feet, if Goliath was typical) of these people. They must have had the blood of demigods running through their veins. But as Israelite religion advanced toward monotheism, the Sons of God were demoted to angels, and their intercourse with mortal women was deemed blasphemous. In *1 Enoch VI, VII, VIII* we are explicitly told that the Sons of God, or Watchers, seduced women, then taught them cosmetics and the arts of seduction in order to induce mortal men, poor creatures, to sin. Satan (here called Semjaza) is made their leader. But *Testament of Reuben 5:5–7* turns it around. Now the women seduce the Sons of God!

The Book of Jubilees 10:11 seems to consider Satan (here called Mastema) one of the demons, sons of the Watchers who fell. Ten per cent are assigned to help him in his appointed task to punish men. *I Enoch 54*, however, says the Watchers sinned by making themselves servants of Satan, already a distinct evil being.

The Apocalypse of Moses 16–17 merges the Genesis 6 story of the Sons of God with the Genesis 3 story of the Garden of Eden, retaining the element of sexual seduction. Now for the first time the serpent is made the innocent dupe, as it were, the demon-possessed mouthpiece of Satan to tempt Eve to sin. In fact it is sexual seduction. And she goes on to seduce Adam into sin. *The Life of Adam and Eve 12–17* explains Satan's motive for this act: he had refused to bow down and do homage before the newly created Adam, so God expelled him from heaven. Satan then decided to show how right he had been about humanity by tempting Adam and Eve. We also find this version in the Koran 7:11–27.

In some manuscripts of *2 Enoch 18:3* "Satanil" is listed as the leader of the fallen angels. This is worth noting, since, whereas "Satan" means "adversary," i.e., of suspected sinners, the suffix "-il" ("God") makes him the "Enemy *of God*." This approaches most closely to the Christian version of Satan. Here he had sought to usurp God's throne in primordial times. His temptation of Eve in Eden is just part of his typical evil-doing.

Ask yourself: if there is such a devil preying upon humans, why did it take so long to build him from various pieces? "Progressive revelation"? Mightn't God have let us in on this threat a bit earlier? And why did the whole picture emerge from a ragtag bunch of apocryphal texts, not in the pages of the Bible?

Who Needs the Devil?[40]

Once, as I was being interviewed for a position at Mount Olive College, the chairman of the Religion Department was going over the institution's Statement of Faith with me. This was the denominational creed I'd be expected to uphold. I was not so far out theologically as I am these days, but still I was a bit wary. I was relieved, however, when Dr. Pelt chuckled as he got to the part about "Satan." Though a staunch Free Will Baptist, he assured me I need not take that particular article of faith too seriously. In fact, I would add, neither does

---

40. With apologies to Manly Wade Wellman, author of "Who Fears the Devil?"

anybody else. Our little tour of Satan's checkered mytho-biography has amply *demon*-strated that, once you've deconstructed the Prince of Darkness, not much is left. You can spot the Frankenstein-seams tenuously binding together his disparate second-hand parts: take God's prosecuting attorney, add an ample helping of the Zoroastrian Ahriman, then a pinch of Philistine Beelzebul, and a cup of the seven-headed Leviathan, then bake at an exceedingly high temperature for a couple of thousand years, and you've got yourself a well-done devil! This is a composite folklore-literary character, like Count Dracula, a mixture of a Hungarian tyrant named Vlad Dracula, of Countess Elisabeth Bathory, and of Varney the Vampire.

But that's not the only reason not to believe in His Satanic Majesty. I'll grant you, he serves as a useful symbol for the evils of this world, shrewdly depicted by Al Pacino in the movie *Devil's Advocate*. There he is a schemer like George Soros, with connections and resources everywhere, doing his deviltry not with infernal miracles but with illegal arms sales and an army of unscrupulous attorneys. But this turns out to be one of those cases of a myth losing its point if you look too closely, because, odd as it sounds, the devil myth implies a naively *optimistic* view of the world! Everything would be hunky-dory if we could just get rid of that Mastermind who is behind all that mischief! Alas, it's nowhere near as simple as that!

Similarly, Satan functions as a scapegoat for human depravity. I remember talking with the saintly Christy Wilson, a Missiology professor at Gordon-Conwell Theological Seminary not long after the Jonestown Horror, the mass suicide of Jim Jones's People's Temple cult in Guyana. Dr. Wilson mused, "Bob, don't you think it was a display of Satan's power?" (or something on that order; I wasn't clandestinely taping him.) My answer: "Actually, no. I think it attested the terrible potential for evil in the human heart." In retrospect, I think my view was more "orthodox" than his! I wasn't willing to minimize the fallenness of human nature. As Brother Jerome says in the great *Twilight Zone* episode, "The Howling Man" (written by

Charles Beaumont): "We don't need *him*" to account for most evils. James apparently didn't think so either: "What causes wars, and what causes fightings among you? Is it not your passions that are at war in your members? You desire and do not have; so you kill. And you covet and cannot obtain; so you fight and wage war."[41] What? No devil?

> Again, to admit the existence of such a being, would be of no avail, as there is nothing for him to do. There is, says the objector; he tempts men to sin. But does he tempt men contrary to their passions and the influence of their motives? Answer, no. Then the temptation is of no possible consequence.[42]

Will the Real Satanists Please Stand Up?

Let me return to that interview, when my department head snickered at the Satan tenet. I imagine he actually *did* think there was a devil, but he saw the irony that a Christian should "believe in" Satan. Doesn't that imply one has *faith in the devil*? Something's wrong there! But in fact, fundamentalists sort of *do* have faith in Satan. They have, without recognizing it, elevated Satan to the exalted state of his Zoroastrian prototype Ahriman, from whom Satan differed in not being a co-equal Power, but rather a treasonous subordinate to Almighty God. But Fundamentalists have restored his full diabolical power! After all, is he not virtually omnipresent? Let me hand it over to Hosea Ballou.[43]

> A created individual being cannot be in more than one place at the same time. But how many *millions* of places must this evil angel be in, at once, in order to perform the business which Christians have

---

41. Sounds like Niebuhr!
42. Ballou, *Treatise on Atonement*, p. 51.
43. Ballou, *Treatise on Atonement*, p. 51.

allotted him? In order for me to believe in such a being, I must give him the omnipresency of the Almighty, which belongs to none, in my opinion, but my Maker.

Fundamentalists and Charismatics often "rebuke Satan" in order to shake off his perceived temptations. Wait a minute—you really think you are addressing Satan? Why is this not to be considered *prayer*? Of course, this is the same issue, really, as when Roman Catholics pray to the Mother of Jesus and numerous saints, even angels. Protestants recoil in horror at this practice, as it implies polytheism. Catholics deny this, pointing to the Apostles' Creed: "I believe in the communion of saints." But isn't that just restating the problem? It is one thing to ask your Christian friend to pray for you. But it is quite another to ask an unseen being up in heaven to pray for you, whether it's the Virgin Mary or your dear departed Aunt Mary.

You may say that, in rebuking the devil, you are just doing what the Lord Jesus did in the wilderness when he told Lucifer to beat it. But Jesus is depicted there as a divine being with habitual intercourse with spiritual entities from the invisible realm. He is on their level. You are not. For him it was a conversation; for you it counts as prayer. Okay, you're not actually *worshipping* the devil, but it would still seem to be prayer, wouldn't it?

Oh the irony! Avowed, explicit Satanists, members of the Temple of Set or of Anton La Vey's Church of Satan *do not believe in the devil*, but delusional Christians are talking to him, telling him to lay off! Maybe they should catch up with the Satanists and, like them, demythologize the devil.

4

Trinitarianism

The Contradictory Compromise

Mileposts along the Evolution of the Doctrine

In the New Testament we have a few sets of "triple" formulae: 2 Corinthians 13:14; 1 Corinthians 12:4–6; Galatians 4:6; 1 Peter 1:2; Ephesians 3:14–16. (We must omit the spurious interpolation 1 John 5:7–8, "For there are three that bear witness in heaven, the Father, the Word, and the Holy Spirit, and these three are one.") Apologists frequently point to these verses and proudly declare on this basis that "the New Testament teaches the doctrine of the Trinity." As both a New Testament scholar and a theologian, I find this shocking and mystifying. Surely it ought to be clear that "sets of three" by no means establish Trinitarianism. This is because the Trinity is a developed philosophical model, and the Bible does not speak in such terms. Now it might be that, if you could get into that time machine you have parked in your garage and go back to the first century CE, explain the Trinity to Paul or John, and ask them if they believed in it, maybe they'd say "yes." I'm not saying they wouldn't. But the Bible leaves the ball in our court. Had Jesus or the apostles taught Trinitarianism, why would it have taken so long for Christian theologians to hammer it out? The raw material of the doctrine, the questions which the Trinity doctrine tries to answer, can be seen emerging in John chapters 14–16, the Johaninne Farewell Discourses.[44] But it is erroneous to claim, as many do, that the Trinity is already present, full-blown, in the New Testament. That is merely the hypocritical assertion of biblicists who *say* they are not at liberty to espouse a belief not spelled out in the New Testament, and it is why the original Socinians and Unitarians rejected Trinitarianism in the Reformation era. But it is more complex than that, as we will shortly see.

Irenaeus at the end of the second century put forth the doctrine of "economic" (or dispensational, or administrative) Trinitarianism. According to this, the three divine persons were first differentiated at creation according to Psalm 33:6 ("By the word of the Lord the heavens were made, and all their host by the breath [*ruach*, "spirit"] of his mouth." Twentieth- century Roman Catholic theologian Piet Schoonenberg[45] made an alternative suggestion, reversing the "enhypostatic humanity" doctrine of Cyril of Alexandria and suggesting instead that the Word first gained its distinct personhood at the incarnation, when it assumed the human being Jesus of Nazareth. The personhood was contributed by the human side, not by the divine, as traditionally, and this implies there was no plurality of persons in the Godhead till the incarnation. The Word and the Spirit had been simply aspects of God till then. Like Irenaeus, Schoonenberg made the Trinity something of a subsequent development.

Marcellinus of Ankyra in the fourth century developed economic Trinitarianism in the direction of *successive* "economies" or "dispensations" of the Logos: first in creation, second in the incarnation, and third in the outpouring of the Spirit at Pentecost. At the Second

---

44. Arthur W. Wainwright, *The Trinity in the New Testament* (London: S.P.C.K., 1962).

45. Piet Schoonenberg, *The Christ: A Study of the God-Man Relationship in the Whole of Creation and in Jesus Christ.* Trans. Della Couling. A Crossroad Book (New York: Seabury Press, 1971).

Coming, he taught, the Logos will again be absorbed into God, and "God will be all in all" (1 Cor. 15:28).

Tertullian in the early third century, in Carthage, introduced the terminology of "three persons, one essence," but by *personae* he meant something like "faces" or "masks," like the ancient actors wore to signify their roles. His meaning might be developed in various ways. Sabellius later in the third century put forth the doctrine of *modalism* (or Patripassianism ["the Father suffers-ism"] or Theopascism ["God suffers-ism"]) which can be seen as a development of Tertullian's ideas. Sabellius said that Father, Son, and Holy Spirit are three *modes* in which God manifests himself, not three persons within the Godhead. The famous "ice-water-steam" analogy fits modalism, not Trinitarianism in its eventual orthodox form.

The Three Cappadocians (Gregory of Nyssa, Gregory of Nazianzus, and Basil of Caesarea) in the fourth century experimented with slightly different terminology: three substances (existences), one essence. This is very close to what became orthodox dogma: "three persons in one essence."

The Councils of Nicea (325) and Constantinople (451) affirmed that the Son and the Spirit were of the same (not just similar) nature with the Father. The later Athanasian Creed made this even more explicit.

Augustine of Hippo in the late fourth century thought of the Trinity in terms of *relations* within a person or between persons. He pictured the Trinity as analogous to memory, intellect, and will, or to lover, beloved, and love. The later controversy between Eastern and Western churches over the addition of the clause *filioque* ("I believe in the Holy Spirit, the Lord, the giver of life, who proceeds from the Father *and from the Son*") to the Nicene-Constantinopolitan Creed is relevant here, since one reason the East rejected it was that they thought having the Spirit proceeding from both Father and Son but *not* proceeding from the Spirit (himself) denigrated the equality of the Spirit with the other two persons. They suspected Western (Augustinian) Trinity analogies did the same by implying that, while the Father and the Son were persons, the Spirit was some kind of impersonal force passing between them.

Roscellinus of York in the eleventh century argued that to speak of "essence" is just to talk about what *kind* of thing something is, what *category* to place it in. The result when applied to the Trinity is that there are three Gods—Tritheism, as (unwittingly) implied in the well-known "three light bulbs" analogy. Mormon theology is, I believe, alone in actually believing in a trio of Gods: Father, Son, and Spirit.

Gregory of Nyssa had already tried to head this objection off by saying that "Godhead" refers to the divine operations or roles, not to nature or essence at all. Jehovah *rules* as God. He is *enthroned* as God. The three persons, Father, Son, and Spirit, all reign as God. And they are of the same nature, just as all human beings are of the same nature with each other and technically ought to be called "man" collectively, never "men" plurally. Granted, we define individuals by their operations of roles, too, and if many do the same thing, we do properly use plurals denoting their roles, like "many orators," "many physicians." They may be distinguished from one another in this way because their work is parallel to or even competitive with one another's. But in the case of God, every act is performed conjointly by all three persons harmoniously, each performing his own function in the performance of the one task, e.g., to save. Thus one cannot distinguish them as "gods" as one could Apollo, Hermes, and Hera, who are (false) gods dividing the labor and doing different things. I confess I am not so sure this works; I think Gregory reads too much into the joint efforts of the members of the Trinity; is this the only reason we may not call them three Gods?

Mystery or Mystification?

Does the Trinity make any sense? Defenders of the doctrine have always admitted that their formulations are not explaining what it means so much as erecting a barrier (a la the *Via Negativa*) to protect the deep truth of the Trinity from the rude and over-simplistic attempts of impatient mortals to whittle it down to some idol they may satisfactorily understand. "Not so fast, mister! There's more to it than you think! Best to fall silent and bask in the Mystery!"

Rationalist theologians like Universalist Hosea Ballou have rejected this, saying that the Trinity is merely a bad theory, and that theologians are just spin doctors trying to cover their butts, making a bad theory look good. Want proof? Ask individual Christians what they think the Trinity means. You will invariably get some sort of modalism or tritheism, not real Trinitarianism, though no one seems to know the difference. And what else can they do? There would seem to be no middle option between the two "heresies" where the would-be orthodox mind may settle down. If you want to believe in a thing, if you want to have some sort of notion in your mind, you are going to "round it off" to one of the options you *can* understand.

Critics[46] charge that the real meaning of the doctrine of the Trinity is this: "*Sit down and shut up!*" That is, it is specifically designed to cut off thought and to cow believers into intimidated submission to Mother Church. "I give up! Go ahead and tell me what to believe! I don't get it, but whatever it means, I'm confident the bishops are right!" This is second-hand "belief." But how can you "believe" in X?

> [Don] Pablo insisted that he believed in a complete unity which has in it a Trinity—which is so profound that even the angels and heavenly hosts cannot comprehend it. . . . Nahmanides replied: "Is it not clear that a person does not believe what he does not comprehend, [and] that, if so, the angels do not believe in the Trinity?"[47]

---

46. Thanks to my good friend Grover Furr for this one!

47. Morris Goldstein, *Jesus in the Jewish Tradition* (New York: Macmillan, 1950), p. 203.

In the end, perhaps the Trinity is less of a doctrine than it is a Zen koan: a riddle that is insoluble by rational cogitation. A koan's purpose is to drive the meditator to the end of his rope, provoking an Alice-like plunge down the rabbit hole to *Satori* (enlightenment).

> The method [Ta-hui] ceaselessly urged on his students was concentrated introspection of the koan, introspection into which not the slightest deliberation or intellectualization entered. The koan was to be introspected deeper and deeper until its full content was revealed.[48]

Since words and intellectual theorizing have not proved very fruitful in grasping the Trinity, maybe it's time for a different approach?

---

48. Isshu Miura and Ruth Fuller Sasaki, *The Zen Koan: Its History and Use in Rinzai Zen*. A Helen and Kurt Wolff Book (New York: Harcourt, Brace & World, 1965), p. 13.

5

Christ-illogical Dogma

Naughty or Nicea

The Virgin Birth

Liberal Protestantism is notorious for its "denial of the Virgin Birth." Since this is liable to be oversimplified as some kind of glib skepticism, it will be helpful to examine why theological Liberals "deny the Virgin Birth." Besides, the Liberal position here is important for understanding the Liberal attitude toward Mariology as a whole.

The Liberal theologian notes the similarity between the New Testament's Virgin Birth stories and several miraculous birth and annunciation stories in ancient legendry. These include the conceptions and/or births of Plato, Alexander, Apollonius of Tyana, Perseus, Augustus, Noah, Moses, Krishna, and the Buddha. The idea is not that the early church directly borrowed from such legends. Rather, we see at work here what Martin Dibelius called "the law of biographical analogy."[49] Thomas Boslooper [50]sums it up:

---

49. Martin Dibelius, *From Tradition to Gospel*. Trans. Bertram Lee Woolf (New York: Scribners, n.d.), p. 108.

50. Thomas Boslooper, *The Virgin Birth* (Philadelphia: Westminster Press, 1962), p. 185.

Similar stories exist in various cultures because of the universal cultural and racial tendency to describe the life of a hero similarly. In the days in which Jesus was born, it was customary for the life of a great man or hero to be embellished with birth narratives.

The critical theologian, then, sees it as likely that the miraculous birth stories of Matthew and Luke are just the kind of legends that would naturally crop up to glorify Jesus. This explanation seems less forced than those of Justin Martyr (such legends are Satanic counterfeits, planted *in advance!*) and C.S. Lewis,[51] that the numerous pre-Christian heroes and saviors were God-inspired anticipations of the coming Christ, virtually prophecies, only with the names changed. (This would seem to contradict what Lewis says elsewhere: "That is one of the reasons I believe in Christianity. It is a religion you could not have guessed."[52])

The Liberal theologian is persuaded that the Matthean and Lukan nativities betray themselves as unhistorical anyway, even if there were no extra-biblical parallels to their miracles. For instance, the two birth stories agree on almost nothing but the birth itself. When each is read on its own, not forcibly harmonized with the other, each has quite a different story to tell. Both want Jesus to be born in Bethlehem but to be called, incongruously, the Nazarene, but here they diverge. Matthew has Mary and Joseph as residents of Bethlehem who only later relocate to Nazareth to escape danger. Luke has them residents of Nazareth who only happen to arrive in Bethlehem for a tax registration when it comes time for Mary to deliver. There are other differences. In Matthew only Joseph receives the annunciation, while in Luke it is only Mary. Luke knows nothing of such momentous events as the slaughter of the innocents by Herod the Great or

---

51. C.S. Lewis, "Myth Became Fact." In Lewis, *God in the Dock: Essays on Theology and Ethics* (Grand Rapids: Eerdmans, 1973), pp. 63–67; Lewis, *Mere Christianity*, p. 54.

52. Lewis, *Mere Christianity*, p. 47.

the subsequent flight into Egypt. Did such "details" simply escape his notice?

Luke's narrative has other signs of being legendary, as when characters burst into inspired song at crucial moments, as in a Broadway musical. The account of the census is a mess, since the first Roman census took place, under Quirinius all right, but 10 years after Jesus was born! And even then it would not have affected Judea, only Galilee.

The nativity stories also seem to contradict traces of a natural birth elsewhere in the New Testament. For instance, the two gospel genealogies seem originally to have assumed that Jesus was the natural son of Joseph. Also, it is difficult to imagine how Mary could have thought Jesus' mission was "mad" (Mark 3:20–21, 31–32) if she had lived through the unforgettable, wondrous events of the nativity stories of Matthew and Luke. Certainly, such considerations do not "prove" the Virgin Birth a legend, but they cast sufficient doubt on it for the Liberal theologian to deem the Virgin Birth a "theological elective." No one should be accused of deficient faith if he doesn't believe in it.

Even if one did not accept the Virgin Birth as a historical fact, couldn't it still be demythologized and regarded as a valid piece of theological symbolism? Some Liberal theologians think so. John Macquarie[53] says, "There is little point in talking about the historicity of the Virgin Birth." "The doctrine of the Virgin Birth is meant to point to Christ's origin in God."

But others do not agree. For various reasons, they find fault with the Virgin Birth even as a theological symbol. Emil Brunner[54] feels that the Virgin Birth is merely a rationalistic attempt to explain the

---

53. Macquarrie, *Principles of Christian Theology*, p. 259.

54. Emil Brunner, *The Mediator: A Study of the Central Doctrine of the Christian Faith*. Trans. Olive Wyon (Philadelphia: Westminster Press, 1957), p. 324–325.

mystery of the Incarnation. Gordon Kaufmann[55] says,

> The doctrine of the so-called virgin birth ... intends to affirm that it is God himself who is here in this man, truly and actually present in his very being. However, it says this crudely, offering a quasi-explanatory account of the matter. ... it turns Jesus into a kind of demi-god—half human, half-divine.

Paul Tillich[56] writes similarly that the symbol of the Virgin Birth "is theologically quasi-heretical. It takes away one of the fundamental doctrines of Chalcedon. ... A human being who has no human father has no full humanity."

Basically, these theologians feel that Jesus' being the Son of God does not at all depend on literal, physical divine paternity. This opinion seems squarely based on a central tenet of New Testament thought. John the Baptist told people that physical descent from Abraham did not guarantee approval from God. The Fourth Gospel uses "virgin birth" language not for Jesus but for those who through faith in him became "children of God" (John 1:12–13). It is spiritual, regardless of physical, descent that constitutes divine Sonship, whether for Jesus or his followers.

The same principle goes far to explain why there is no Mariology in Liberal Protestant theology. "Apollo has no revelatory significance for Christians; the Virgin Mary reveals nothing to Protestants" (Paul Tillich).[57] Liberals reject any real theological importance for Mary since to glorify her would be to make too much of physical, merely natural ties. This general principle is applied already in the New Testament to Jesus' mother (Luke 11:27–28). Since the birth narratives

---

55. Gordon Kaufman, *Systematic Theology: A Historicist Perspective* (New York: Scribners, 1968), p. 203.

56. Paul Tillich, *Theology of Culture*, (Chicago: University of Chicago Press, 1959), p. 66.

57. Paul Tillich, *Systematic Theology*, vol. I, p. 128.

probably do not give us any real biographical information about Mary, what basis can there be for glorifying her other than the sheer fact of maternity? Besides, even if Mary's humble obedience to God were known to be historical fact, this virtue would hardly place her on a higher level than other biblical figures like Abraham. (Compare Luke 1:48 with Mark 14:9).

Tillich expresses another decisive difficulty with Mariology. The Virgin Mary is "a symbol which has died in Protestantism by [virtue of] the changed situation of the relationship to God. The special, direct, immediate relationship to God makes a mediating power [on Mary's part] impossible."[58] She can no longer be venerated, as in Catholicism, as a mediator with God. (Nor is that a caricature, since Catholics have referred to Mary as Co-Redemptrix, even Co-Creatrix.)

And, as Heiko Oberman[59] points out, the Catholic Mariological dogma of the *"homo purus,"* or "genuine humanity" of Mary tends to minimize the real humanity of Jesus. Mary is "contrasted with Christ who is not *homo purus* but *homo deus*. Christ is not pure nature because his humanity is united in hypostatic union with the Godhead. In contrast to Mary, Christ did not, therefore, really and fully belong to mankind." Such an implication of Mariology would indeed severely contradict the central Liberal Protestant thrust: the completely natural humanity of Jesus.

The Development of Christology

Some early Christians believed that Jesus Christ was a supremely righteous man who had been adopted by God, either at his baptism (Mark 1:11) or at the resurrection (Acts 2:36; Rom. 1:3–4). They are called *adoptionists*. Others believed Christ was a divine Spirit or an-

---

58. Tillich, *Theology of Culture,* p. 65.

59. Heiko Oberman, *The Virgin Mary in Evangelical Perspective.* Facet Books Historical Series 20 (Fortress Press, 1971), p. 20.

gel who only seemed to appear in human flesh (Rom. 8:3; Phil. 2:8; 1 John 4:2; 2 John 7). They are called *docetists* (from the Greek *dokeo*, "to seem"). The mildest form of docetism merely denied that the dying Jesus suffered any pain. A stronger form denied that Jesus died there at all, his place being taken by another man or by a false vision of Jesus. The Koran inherited this version from Christians who might have read it in the Acts of John or the Nag Hammadi Apocalypse of Peter. The strongest version, also attested in the Acts of John, is that Jesus had no real human form at all, with different people simultaneously seeing him differently.

Still others believed that the Christ-Spirit/angel entered into the man Jesus at the latter's baptism (Mark 1:10, literally, "descended into him") and departed at his crucifixion (Mark 15:34), and in the meantime, Jesus was the channeler for the Christ. Bart Ehrman[60] calls this *separationism* (1 Cor. 12:31; John 2:22). All these views were eventually condemned as heresies, which by no means stopped people from believing in them. But the evolving establishment Church, beginning with Constantine, took up the matter in a series of debates and councils, which we will survey. In all of them the pendulum kept trying to settle in the middle between Jesus as a man and Jesus as divine.

The Arian Controversy

The Nicene Creed was drafted to resolve the Christological controversy between the Arians (Arius, Asterius, Eusebius of Nicomedia) and the Alexandrians (Bishops Alexander and Athanasius). Neither of their Christological positions was identical with what would later emerge as "orthodoxy." *Athanasius* held that Jesus Christ was the Word made flesh (John 1:14). The Word (Logos, the creative reason of God, a notion derived from Heraclitus, the Stoics, and Philo) was a separate person sharing the divine nature. The Word is also the Son. The Father begat or generated the Son, but this is a logical, not

---

60. Ehrman, *Orthodox Corruption of Scripture*, p. xii.

a chronological, priority. They have always been in a relationship of loving interdependence: the Son is "eternally begotten" by the Father, as Origen said. Lewis[61] compares it to two books, one resting upon the other, but no one ever put the one on top of the other: they have *always* been in that position. But this absurd notion simply repeats rather than resolving the conundrum.

The Word is God's own wisdom through which he created all things (Prov. 8; John 1:1–3). The Son took on human flesh (not yet understood as a full human nature, just a human body, which will later be considered heresy) in order to save humanity.

Arius held that Jesus Christ was the incarnation of a heavenly being who had been the very first creature, and through whom as an agent or assistant God had created the rest of the creation (Wis. 8:22; Sir. 1:4; Col. 1:15–16). But he did not share divine nature, the nature of the Father. Both before and during his earthly sojourn he learned wisdom and virtue through discipline and suffering. At the resurrection he was given divine honor and dignity. He was adopted *by grace* as "Son," "Word," "Lord," "Wisdom," even "God," because by his perfection in virtue he had come to participate in these qualities which *by nature* belong to God alone. God's foreknowledge told him from the beginning that Christ would successfully attain this perfection, and so scripture calls Christ "Son," "Word," "God," etc., by anticipation even before his earthly life (e.g., John 1:1; Gal. 4:4).

Arians offered two chief lines of argument: First, there are *three scriptural points* to be made. The outline of this schema of Christ being pre-existent in heaven, yet later receiving even greater glory as a reward, is certainly to be found in Philippians 2:5–11 and in the Epistle to the Hebrews. The idea that the pre-existent Word as an agent of creation was himself created can easily be inferred from John 1:1 ("and the Word was divine" or "the Word was a god.") since the created status of Wisdom is explicit in the texts that clearly form

---

61. Lewis, *Mere Christianity*, pp. 150–151.

the background of John 1. The notion of Christ's being perfected through endurance and suffering and of growing in wisdom is found in Luke 2:52 and in Hebrews 2:10.

Second, there are *three theological points*. The idea of the Father begetting the Word smacked of Gnostic emanationism. If the Word were eternal, he must be unbegotten, and this would seem to make Christ into God's *brother*, not his Son! "Eternal generation" is a piece of incoherent sophistry, like a "square circle." And if God is Father *by nature*, and if the Son is Son *by nature*, then God was *forced* to beget the Son, and this is to reject God's sovereignty and freedom.

The Central Issue: Soteriology

Both sides understood salvation as *theosis*, divinization or deification. Christ had made it possible for us to "become God." Athanasius said, "God became man so that man might become God." We could become immortal. By grace, i.e., by adoption, we could become what God is by nature. In order to attain this, we must live a life of faith and good works. This remains the Eastern Orthodox view, where they preach unabashedly the doctrine of *synergism*: we must work with God for our salvation.

Athanasius held that Christ must be identified with God in order to make our deification possible. Human nature is mortal/corruptible because it is subject to change and decay (including moral decay, or sin). *Theosis*, deification of human nature, is made possible because in Christ's incarnation the unchanging eternal, divine nature unites with human nature and transforms it essentially. In Christ we experience this transformation. Christ must have been God incarnate, since otherwise the savior could not bring to humanity what humanity needs for deification: genuine deity. By contrast, Arius believed that Christ must be identified with creatures in order to make our deification possible: Christ, *precisely as a creature*, attains the reward of deification in exactly the same way we do ("the pioneer and perfector of our faith;" "the firstborn of many brothers") and thus establishes the possibility of deification for the rest of us creatures. No alchemy of essences and natures is needed; God simply effects the adoption as sons/daughters by his grace, i.e., by fiat.

The Council of Nicea, in 325, summoned by Constantine, decided the issue by voting in Athanasius' favor. After the Emperor's death, the decision was reversed, then reversed again, so that the initially victorious Athanasius was suddenly exiled, then recalled! Arian Christology, the belief that Jesus Christ was not fully God *or* man, but a kind of archangel, survived among the barbarian Goths, evangelized by the Arian missionary Ulfilas. They lived in Northern Europe from whence many later relocated to North Africa. Early passages of the Koran seem perhaps to reflect Arian Christology, and many Arian Christians converted to Islam. Today the major Arian group is Jehovah's Witnesses. Arian Christology has also remained a favorite notion among certain English theologians.[62]

Next came the *Apollinarian Controversy*. The aftermath of the Arian Controversy was the debate over precisely how human Jesus Christ was, granting that he possessed full divinity. Athanasius had pretty much taken the humanity of Jesus for granted without defining it. His disciple *Apollinarius* taught what he believed to be the natural implication of Athanasius' doctrine, namely that Jesus Christ had only a human body of flesh and a human soul/mind, but not a human *spirit*. That, he reasoned, must have been "left open" to fit in the divine Logos. After all, it had to plug into the organism *someplace*, right?

He was opposed by three theologians (boyhood chums, now ecclesiastical bigwigs): *Gregory of Nyssa*, *Gregory of Nazianzus*, and *Basil of Caesarea*, all from the Asia Minor province of Cappadocia, hence their collective nickname, the *Three Cappadocians*. (We have met them before.) These men argued that if Jesus saved us by

---

62. Maurice Wiles, *Archetypal Heresy: Arianism through the Centuries* (New York: Oxford University Press, 1996).

merely Christianity

becoming human, assuming humanity (i.e., taking humanity onto himself), and so raising us to the level of divinity, then in order to save our spirits he must have *had* a human spirit, not just the divine one. What, did he redeem only two thirds of a human being? Their formula was "What is not assumed is not redeemed." So Jesus Christ must have been fully human as well as fully divine, not half and half like a mythical demigod.

The Council of Constantinople decided this issue in favor of the Three Cappadocians in 381. While they promulgated no new creed, they did beef up the original draft of the Nicene Creed, adding extra material about the Holy Spirit ("the Lord, the giver of life, who proceeds from the Father"), so that the version repeated in churches today is actually the Nicene-Constantinopolitan Creed.

The Nestorian Controversy was the next installment. The story goes that Nestorius, Bishop of Constantinople, was disturbed at hearing some of his parishioners chanting the praises of Mary as the *Theotokos*, Mother of God. This made him reflect upon the Christological question: how are the divine and human natures of Jesus Christ related? He decided they could not be related in a way that would make it meaningful to call Mary's infant son "God." He is said to have exclaimed, "God is not a baby two or three months old!" Imagine the scene at home with the Holy Family: "Mary, cantcha change God's diaper?" "Joseph, it's time for the Almighty's two o'clock feeding!" In the once-controversial French film *Hail Mary*, which sets the nativity in the modern world, the Holy Family is setting off for a picnic in the country when all of a sudden, out of nowhere, young Jesus announces, to no apparent point, "I am he who is." Joseph's reaction: "Get in the car."

Nestorius was thought to have taught something to the effect that in Jesus Christ there were two subjects, divine and human, perhaps two persons, or something close to this. According to his own rediscovered writings, admittedly not a model of clarity, Nestorius regarded Jesus of Nazareth as "the assumed Man," and there was the divine Word, the pre-incarnate Son of God. By the grace of God they formed one person with two natures. But Nestorius was misrepresented as teaching that Jesus and the Word were two persons sharing but a moral unity. "Opposing" him (but actually holding to virtually the same view!) was Cyril of Alexandria who argued that Jesus had been one person with two natures (divine and human) and that the personhood was divine, supplied from the divine side, in that, had there been no mission of incarnation for the Word to undertake, there should have been no Jesus of Nazareth at all. The divine Word forms the nucleus of the Incarnation. This sounds sort of like Apollinarianism, but it isn't, since Cyril readily admits the human Jesus had a body, soul, and spirit. He was fully human, though he wouldn't have existed at all except for his divine destiny. On the other hand, it is not hard to see how Nestorius' position might be taken as opening the door to a kind of adoptionism or separationism. It bothered Cyril and his faction that Nestorians spoke of a "Word/man" Christology, not a "Word/flesh" Christology.

The Council of Ephesus decided in 431 in favor of Cyril. Of course this didn't really settle much; the Nestorian churches just picked up their marbles and left for home. Nestorian Christianity still thrives today, especially in Iran. Nestorius had been vilified, made a strawman against which to define orthodoxy. He did not actually espouse what is called "the Nestorian heresy," nor do today's Nestorians. In fact, one photograph of a gathering of Nestorians shows them holding up a big banner praising the Theotokos!

The Monophysite Controversy began when Eutyches, pious Archimandrite of a monastery in Constantinople, tried to explain how the two natures of Christ were related in one person. He admitted that the divine and human natures remained distinct from one another going into the union, until the point of the incarnation, the impregnation of Mary. Afterward, Eutyches ventured, the two natures combined into a single nature (*monos physis*), unique to Jesus Christ. From thereon in Christ has a single nature. One person *from* two natures. The implied analogy is like salt and water: they fuse together into a new, single solution. Those who believe this are known as "Monophysites."

Opposing Eutyches was Pope Leo, among others, Leo being the actual author of the formal response to Monophysitism, *Leo's Tome*. These Dyophysites (believers in two natures) insisted that the two natures remained distinct, inseparably united, not mingled or confused. The proper analogy here would be that of oil and water: pour both into a blender and run it till Doomsday, and the oil is never going to mix with the water, even though not so much as a film of oxygen molecules separates them.

The Council of Chalcedon decided this one in favor of Leo and his compatriots in 451. Again, there was no actual resolution, since the numerous Monophysite churches went their merry way and exist till this very day. The Coptic Church, the Ethiopian Orthodox Church, the Armenian Orthodox Church, etc., are Monophysite. (I once went to hear a speech by the Coptic Pope Shenouda III—before Anwar Sadat threw him into prison!)

I recall how, once during a high school youth retreat I bought a little book on Church History published by ultra-conservative Moody Press. I read it with interest till I came to the chapter on the Christological councils I just discussed above. A naïve fundamentalist kid, I was shocked to find that things were not so simple as I been led to believe! You mean it wasn't true that Jesus told the disciples he was God incarnate, and that was that? You mean it took hundreds of years for the dogma to be debated and defined—by majority vote? What the hell? That pretty much proves that Jesus hadn't explained any of this. Nowadays the aspect of the whole process that strikes me as the most damning is the fact that, at these councils, the bishops were really *creating* the incarnation, extrapolating what *had* to have been the case with Jesus for their theology to work. It was like the colonial patriots getting together to draft the Declaration of Independence and, later, the Constitution.

It is so easy to take these things for granted. But it's certainly understandable, at least once you read Berger and Luckmann,[63] who explain how all institutions begin as human inventions but soon take on a life of their own. The founders, the framers, the fathers are fully aware that they are creating something: a system of government, a corporation, a game with rules of play. They know it has less factual reality than they as individual persons do. But as soon as a new generation is raised up to inherit their predecessors' invention, they can't help regarding it very differently. It is perceived as having an authoritative and venerable *givenness*, as if it were a fact of nature rather than of history, of culture. The state, the church, the corporation, was meant to serve them, but they serve it. "The Sabbath was made for man, not man for the Sabbath." With this in mind, picture the bishops returning home from the Council of Nicea: did they, could they, have really *felt* they now *knew* the truth about Jesus Christ, the immortal Logos who shares the same nature of the Father? Was the Nicene Creed, for its framers, a list of "doctrines felt as facts"?[64] Not just a paper agreement like a contract or a treaty? I doubt it, but it seemed that way to all subsequent generations.

In short, the resultant Christology was a human invention, not a divine revelation. It was merely Christianity.

---

63. Peter L. Berger and Thomas Luckmann *The Social Construction of Reality: A Treatise in the Sociology of Knowledge* (Garden City: Doubleday Anchor Books, 1967), pp. 58–59.

64. Dennis Nineham, *The Use and Abuse of the Bible: A Study of the Bible in an Age of Rapid Cultural Change*. Library of Philosophy and Religion (New York: Barnes & Noble Books, 1976), p. 25.

6

The Holy Ghost

Caboose of the Trinity

There is much, and yet little, to be said about the Holy Ghost. In the Old Testament, the activity of the Holy Spirit is depicted as a comparatively rare and dramatic event. It comes upon some individuals appointed for special tasks, e.g., the Judges were given an anointed commission for leadership (Judg. 3:10; 6:34; 11:29; 13:25; 15:14). Samson was also given superhuman strength by the Spirit of Jehovah. The most outstanding activity prompted by the Spirit was prophecy. Prophets were divinely inspired spokesmen for God, delivering his messages and ultimatums to individuals and countries (Ezek. 11:5; 2 Chron. 15:1; 24:20). But Elijah and Elisha also did miracles by the Spirit's power. Prophesying also sometimes describes an individual or group being in some kind of inspired or ecstatic state because of the Spirit's visitation (1 Sam. 10:3–13; 19:20–24; Num. 11:25–30; cf. Luke 1:41–42, 67ff; 2:25–32).

At first, there was no hope for a wider distribution of the Spirit (Num. 11:30), but eventually the prophets themselves began to hint at greater things to come. One day all the faithful will have their share of the Spirit (Isa. 32:15; 44:3; Ezek. 36:25–27; 39:29; Zech. 12:10; Joel 2:28ff.). The glorified Jesus pours out the Spirit to his people (John 7:39; 15:26; Acts 2:33). This is seen by the New Testament writers as the fulfillment of the prophetic promise (John 7:38b-39 NIV marginal reading; Acts 2:16; Eph. 1:13). But since the prophetic predictions placed the coming of the Spirit in an eschatological context, the Spirit's coming itself functions as a promise for the future. It is the beginning of the arrival of the end-times blessings. Since the believer now experiences the phenomenal reality of the Spirit, he is sure that he will soon experience the rest of the end-times manifestations, e.g., bodily resurrection or transfiguration at the Parousia. As such a guarantee (Eph. 1:14), the Spirit is variously characterized as, e.g., "first fruits," "down payment," and as a seal of ownership (Rom. 5:2-5; 8:23; Eph. 1:13; 4:30; Heb. 6:4-5; 1 John 4:13; 2 Cor. 1:22; 5:5). Similarly, Peter appeals to the coming of the Spirit as a sign of the impending end (Acts 2:16-17, 20, 40, "This is that spoken of by the prophet Joel: 'And in these last days . . . before the Day of the Lord comes. . . . Save yourselves from this crooked [doomed] generation'").

The chief function of the end-time Spirit spoken of in Joel, and in the New Testament as well, is that of *prophecy*. The coming of the Spirit for Joel results in all God's servants speaking as prophets in various ways (Joel 2:28). Jesus predicts that the Spirit will inspire supernatural wisdom to refute accusers and opponents (Matt. 10:19-20; Mark 13:11; John 16:7-11), a promise which is fulfilled in Acts 4:8, 29-31; 6:9-10; 13:9-11. He also promises encouragement (the Spirit as "Paraclete," cf. 1 Cor. 14:3; Acts 4:36; 11:24; 13:1), power for effective witness (Acts 1:8; 4:31; John 15:26-27; cf. 1 Cor. 14:24-25; 1 Thes. 1:5; 1 Peter 1:12; 4:10-11; 2 Tim. 1:7), and further revelation of truth (John 16:12-13; cf. Eph. 3:3ff; 1 Cor. 14:16-26 ["revelation"]; Rom. 16:25-26). Most notably, however, the Spirit's coming issues in ecstatic praise (Acts 2:1-4;10:46; 19:6; 1 Cor. chapters 12-14; Mark 16:17; Rom. 8:26; Eph. 5:18-20; Jude 20) and intelligible prophecy (Acts 11:27-28; 13:2; 21:9-11; 1 Cor. 14:29-32; 1 Thes. 5:14-21; 1 Peter 4:10-11).

John the Baptist had promised the Spirit to those who would re-pent and prove it by bearing ethical fruit. He thought that the Spirit would come at the very End. By Paul's time, the eschatological per-spective has changed, so that the Spirit is seen to be operative even before the final climax. This allows him to develop Jeremiah's con-necting of the Spirit with a new covenant of obedience. The Spirit transfers God's law to our hearts (2 Cor. 3:3; Rom. 2:15) with the result that we serve in the newness of the Spirit, rather than by the written code (Rom. 7:6; 2 Cor. 3:6). What Paul sees that John the Baptist did not see was that the Spirit itself enables us to bear the fruit expected of those who hope to enter the kingdom of God (Gal. 5:19–23). The Spirit, then, prepares us to face the Final Judgment (1 Cor. 1:7–9; 2 Cor. 3:18; Phil. 1:6; Col. 1:27–29; 1 Thes. 3:12–13; Eph. 5:26–27; 1 John 4:13–17; 1 Pet. 1:2, 5).

How does one receive the Spirit? Since the epistles generally assume that their readers have already received the Spirit (1 Cor. 12:13; Gal. 5:25a), they contain no statements describing how this happens. One can only surmise that the reception of the Spirit was pretty fundamental, occurring (like baptism in water) early on in the Christian experience. Our only hints as to when and how the Spirit was initially experienced by converts will be found in the Acts of the Apostles. Here we find that Spirit-baptism (= receiving the Spirit, filling with the Spirit, having the Spirit come upon one) is ap-parently connected with water-baptism. Both *follow* faith in Jesus. They are considered to be *inseparable* from faith (and each other) but are not *identical* to faith (and each other). In other words, wa-ter- and Spirit-baptism are always expected of converts, but they are actions that must *be taken* by converts (or *done to them*, i.e., by another human being) following upon their act of belief. This is not the same as the modern idea that belief in and of itself automatically brings the Spirit, so that a believer is, *ipso facto*, automatically one who experiences the Spirit. In the New Testament, Spirit-baptism is something all believers are assumed to have experienced, but they had to appropriate it, e.g., by the laying on of hands.

Similarly, Paul says that, "if anyone does not have the Spirit of Christ, he does not belong to Christ" (Rom. 8:9). His meaning is clarified in an accompanying statement (8:14) where we see that "having the Spirit" is tantamount to repeatedly appropriating the "leading of the Spirit" (in the same way that "belonging to Christ" is parallel to "being sons of God"). Paul doesn't mean the moment of faith immediately brings the Spirit. Rather, all believers, because of the church's practice, may be assumed to have received the Spirit (just as they may be assumed to have been baptized in water). Paul's tracing of membership in the Body of Christ and of salvation to the Spirit and/or to water baptism (Rom. 6:4; Titus 3:5; 1 Cor. 12:13; Gal. 5:25a) comes from his awareness that all converts were soon immersed and had the laying on of hands for the Spirit. Likewise in Acts, Spirit-baptism is considered as practically contemporaneous with belief (Acts 11:16–17) but is seen to occur (normally) via a ritual *following* (even if by only an interval of minutes) faith and baptism (Acts 19:5–6).

In the case of the Samaritan Christians, the interval between faith and the Spirit is much longer, even though water-baptism has already occurred (8:16). The Pentecost pilgrims are told to believe and (then) be baptized, and (then) receive the Spirit (2:38). The Ephesian sectarians are initially assumed to be Christians who may nevertheless not have the Spirit *yet* (19:2), though Paul will gladly close this gap. Cornelius and his group (Acts chapter 10) receive the Spirit first (even before an explicit "decision" for Christ!) and are baptized following this, since without the evidence of the Spirit, Peter would have been unwilling to baptize them in water (10:44–48). In short, Spirit-baptism does not seem to have been automatic upon belief, but rather *ritually appropriated* following (usually right after) belief. Since water- and Spirit-baptism normally accompanied belief, both could be described as the source of salvation, as by synecdoche, a part standing for the whole.

If the New Testament does not accord with modern evangelical thought that the Spirit is automatically received, *neither does it agree that the continuing experience of the Spirit is automatic and uninterrupted.* First, turning again to Luke-Acts, it seems that the "democratization" of the Spirit does not mean that believers have the Spirit all the time instead of intermittently as did the pre-Christian pneumatics (Luke 1:41–42, 67ff; 2:25–32), but rather that the scope of the number who possess the Spirit (intermittently) is widened to *all* the faithful. Peter and the 120 are filled with the Spirit at Pentecost and again later on (Acts 4:31). If we do not read into the text the modern distinction between "indwelling" and "filling" of the Spirit, it becomes evident that, *for Luke, the Spirit comes and goes* even in the New Covenant age of the Spirit, though there are *(only) some who seem to be constantly "full of the Spirit,"* i.e., especially holy (Acts 6:3; 11:24; cf. Luke 1:15).

Similarly, Paul says that a Christian must "walk by" or "be led by" the Spirit (Rom. 8:14) or he is no son of God. But this comes about by repeatedly deciding to "sow to the Spirit" (Gal. 6:8) and being "filled with the Spirit" (Eph. 5:18) again and again, that is, appropriating it (just as the *Sitz-im-Leben Kirche* [65] of Luke 11:5–13 presupposes a *persistent pleading for the Spirit by believers*).

In the context of prophetic manifestations of the Spirit, Paul also sees repeated "givings" of the Spirit. "Gifts" are not powers or ministries permanently bestowed on individuals, but rather are specific acts of manifestation of the Spirit coming upon individuals in the modes of glossolalia, prophecy, healing, etc. The Spirit (wind) blows where it will, distributed according to his will (John 3:8; Acts 2:3; 1 Cor. 12:4–11). In this perspective it is interesting that Paul's readers have experienced the Spirit (Eph. 1:13), yet he prays that they may yet receive the Spirit of revelation and urges them to be repeatedly filled with the Spirit in order to offer charismatic praise (Eph.

---

65 Life-setting in the Church, subsequent to Jesus.

5:18–19). Likewise, the case of Timothy is interesting. He is already a "disciple" when Paul meets him (Acts 16:1) but receives the Spirit at Paul's hands (2 Tim. 1:6–7) and is told to fan into flame that (latent) gift.

The Spirit and Personality

The Spirit of Yahweh in the Old Testament seems to have been conceived of as the present power of God at work in the midst of his people. Similarly, the Spirit is the miraculous effusion of power from God enabling Jesus (and his apostles) to work wonders (Acts 10:38). Once Jesus is glorified, it is *his* personal presence that is conveyed by the Spirit. The Spirit is "another Comforter" (John 14:16), yet this seems to imply but another mode of presence for Jesus himself, who first "dwells with" the disciples and then "shall be in" them (John 14:17). Similarly, in Acts the "Spirit of Jesus" (16:7) poured out by Jesus upon his disciples seems to be the continued presence of Jesus in his Church, guiding and directing his servants. His word of command comes equally through post-ascension appearances (Acts 9:4–6, 10–16) and prophecies from the Spirit (10:19–20;13:2). As the Gospel according to Luke was the record of what "Jesus *began* to do and teach," so Acts is the record of what he *continued* to do and teach through/as the Spirit. Even so, it is the same for Jesus and for the Spirit to inspire wisdom before persecutors (compare Luke 21:14–15 with Luke 12:11–12). For Paul, too, to have (or to be in) Christ is to have (or to be in) the Spirit. In fact, Jesus "became a life-giving Spirit" (1 Cor. 15:45) and "fills all in all" (Eph. 1:23). The angel sent by Jesus to his servant John on Patmos is also identified as "the Spirit" (Rev. 2:11, 17, 29, etc.) and speaks in the name of "the Son of God" (2:18). All of this points to the New Testament identification of the Spirit as the mode by which the exalted Jesus is personally present to his Church, just as the Old Testament pictured the Spirit as the vehicle for Yahweh's presence among Israel. Thus the Bible seems not so much concerned with the Spirit being "a person" as with it being *the mode of God's being personal to his people.*

Whence comes the idea of the "personality of the Holy Spirit"? The Worldwide and International Church of God movements (the churches of Herbert W. Armstrong and Garner Ted Armstrong respectively) hold to binitarianism, which is like Trinitarianism except that it rejects the personality of the Spirit. Others consider them heretics for it. Where did the idea come from? The Bible seems not to speak of personality in connection with the Spirit except insofar as the Spirit bears the personality of Christ to us. The "person" or "substance" idea of Tertullian and the Cappadocians does not suggest something quite so specific in meaning as our modern notion of "person" or "personality." Nor even does Augustine's analogy of relations within a person. "Person" was defined more in our sense, and applying it to the Trinity, by Boethius in the sixth century. Henceforth "person" denotes at least an individual center of rationality.[66]

Paraclete or Parakeet?

The only visible manifestation of the Spirit in the New Testament is as a bird, or as Luke has it, "in bodily form as a dove," which seems to imply physical substance, suggesting a parallel of sorts with Vishnu's avatars as a swan, a fish, a tortoise, and a boar.[67] Mark has Jesus perceive the descent of the Spirit in a post-baptismal vision: "he saw

---

66. See Hermann Gunkel, *The Influence of the Holy Spirit* (Philadelphia: Fortress Press, 1979); Hendrikus Berkhof, *The Doctrine of the Holy Spirit* (Richmond: John Knox Press, 1967); James D.G. Dunn, *Jesus and the Spirit: A Study of the Religious and Charismatic Experience of Jesus and the First Christians as Reflected in the New Testament* (London: SCM Press, 1974); (Philadelphia: Westminster Press, 1976).

67. Geoffrey Parrinder, *Avatar and Incarnation*. The Wilde Lectures in Natural and Comparative Religion at Oxford University (London: Faber and Faber, 1970), pp. 23–24. These avatars were originally mythic creatures without reference to Vishnu but were later enshrined in the roster of his incarnations because of their legendary feats of rescue. One wonders, then, if Rin Tin Tin and Lassie might have been avatars, too!

The Holy Ghost 73

the heavens opened and the Spirit descending into him like a dove." Matthew makes a change: now the Spirit does not enter into him but only "rests upon him," no doubt in order to avoid the Gnosticizing implications of Mark's "into him." John's gospel does not have Jesus baptized, and he makes John the Baptist, not Jesus, see the Spirit descending and remaining on Jesus (1:32–33), presumably on his shoulder. (If Disney ever makes a cartoon version of Luke, you may rest assured they will have the divine dove accompany Jesus as his little pal, making clever remarks to him throughout the story.)

John's farewell discourses have Jesus predicting the coming of the Paraclete (advocate, councilor), and here he, the Spirit of Truth, does sound like a person analogous to Jesus, his replacement once Jesus ascends to heaven. I believe Bultmann[68] has it right when he ventures the suggestion that John intends the Paraclete as a human being, a follow-up to Jesus arriving to set forth a fuller, even esoteric version of Jesus' teaching. Here Bultmann has tapped into a wider pattern recurring in Near-Eastern religions whereby God sends re-vealers in pairs. First comes "the Proclaimer" to preach the public, exoteric version, followed shortly by "the Foundation," who provides the deeper, esoteric version for the illuminati.[69] Marcionites took Paul to be the Paraclete (which is pretty much the Protestant view if you think about it!), while the Montanists shared the Paraclete role among Montanus and his colleagues Priscilla and Maximilla. Muslims regarded Muhammad as the Paraclete, though appearing long after Jesus. The Ismaili Shi'ite version was as follows: first Adam, then Seth; first Noah, then Shem; first Moses, then Aaron; first Je-sus, then Peter; first Muhammad, then Ali, and so on. The eleventh-

68. Rudolf Bultmann, *The Gospel of John, A Commentary*. Trans. G.R. Beasley-Murray, R.W.N. Hoare, and J.K. Riches (Philadelphia: Westminster Press, 1971), p. 567.

69. Sami Nasib Makarem, *The Doctrine of the Ismail'is*. Islamic Series (Bei-rut: Arab Institute for Research and Publishing, 1972), pp, 29–34; Farhad Daftary, *The Ismail'is: Their History and Doctrines* (New York: Cambridge University Press, 1990), pp. 89, 139.

century Druze faith,[70] which taught that the Fatimid caliph of Egypt, al-Hakim, was Allah incarnate, was proclaimed initially by one al-Hamzah, then given its esoteric elaboration by a "heretical" missionary named ad-Darazi (from whom the name "Druze" derives).

Who, then, would have been John's candidate for the job? Of course, the Paraclete is the Fourth Evangelist himself, represented in the gospel narrative as the so-called Beloved Disciple. This is why John's Jesus sounds so very unlike the Synoptic Jesus of Matthew, Mark, and Luke. We are really hearing the voice of the Paraclete, he who was to reveal to the disciples those more advanced truths for which they were not yet ready while Jesus was among them (John 16:12–15). Look at it this way: now, dear reader, *you* are privy to the esoteric truth!

---

70. Sami Nasib Makarem, *The Druze Faith* (Delmar, NY: Caravan Books, 1974), pp. 71–72.

7

The Pratfall of Man[71]
Doing What Comes Naturally

Why did God create? One often hears that God created a world to share his love and goodness. This is distinct from saying that he was lonely and wanted company. For one thing, according to the classical divine attribute of *aseity*, God cannot have wanted for anything, can have felt no deprivation. For another, if one posits the Trinity, God was already something of an interactive, loving fellowship. It is important in any case to avoid saying that God created out of some *need*, if only the need to create. And yet this is important only as long as we wish to see God as a person who has a will, for then we must avoid saying that his will is compelled or directed, since that would mean there is some force mightier than him. God, to be sovereign, must be free.

But one might follow Benedict Spinoza and say that God, being infinite, cannot be burdened with the limitations that constitute personality (aren't personalities unique because of their particular combinations of particular traits among all those available?). So the infinite God is beyond personality. Spinoza was a Pantheist, understanding God to be the divine nature of all things equally, not a Su-

---

71. I'm stealing this line from my hilarious and erudite pal Ed Babinski.

preme Being, a Supreme Thing among and above created things. In this case, while we cannot suppose there was ever a time when the (divine) universe was not here, we have to affirm that its constant changing evolution and development are all inevitably, ineluctably, the logical outworking of the nature of God, though from our worm's eye view we cannot grasp what that may be. Thus "God" *is* required by "his" nature to "create."

In Advaita Vedanta Hindu theology, God creates the universe as an act of sheer play (*laya*). This is, I think, another way of describing grace, the spontaneity or gratuity of divine action. In the same way, the Krishna stories present a kindred view of "theodicy" (explanation of why adversity plagues us in a God-controlled world): Lord Krishna is playing tricks on us! In other words, there is a randomness about events, and yet we still live in a sacred cosmos.

The Fall and Human Nature

Was there a point in time when humanity sinned and became permanently alienated from God? When human nature became depraved or at least morally impotent? How much of a watershed was the Fall? Was it the derailment of God's creation? Or was it a part of the process of creation?

One's view of the Fall into sin is shaped not so much by one's view of human nature but rather by one's view of the limitations of the religious life. How much do we expect of the regenerate life? Pietists who seek to maintain a constant level of advanced sanctification, a victorious Christian life, a Spirit-filled life, etc., are more inclined to view this type of life as the norm and a worldly, "carnal" life as a substandard, deplorable condition. For them, as they look back on the Fall, it seems to them a tragic disaster from which only piecemeal recovery (as individuals become converted and sanctified) is possible, that is, before the Parousia (Second Coming) of Christ. Such holy folks feel less at home in this world, more restless for heaven. On the other hand, more world-affirming religious folks (Jews, Episcopalians, Catholics, etc.) tend to agree with Tillich[72] in seeing the Fall as part of the Creation story: together they form the whole story of who we are and how we got this way (whether you take the Eden story literally or as a profound psychological myth). This means the normative human condition is a worldly, fleshly, less heavenly-minded, though still wholesome existence. Jews speak of the "evil imagination" (*yetzer harah*) that brings temptation, lust, rage, cruelty, etc., but which we ought not to be in a hurry to eradicate from ourselves lest we find ourselves without the backbone to be tough on evildoers, without the libido to reproduce the species, etc. As the Psalm says, "He knoweth our frame, that we are dust." In other words, God commands repentance, but he is merciful, too, because as our Creator, he knows full well the pitiful stuff we are made of. We wouldn't be human without sin. This view is more compatible with a particular view of the church as "a school for sinners" (St. Cyprian), while the other is more of a sectarian "camp of the saints" model.[73]

It is equally important to understand that Christianity views the ramifications of the Fall as much more severe than Judaism does, not because of a more acute diagnosis of the human condition, but rather because of the Christian doctrine of the atonement of Christ. Think of it this way: if sin was "only" as serious as Judaism makes it, if it is a matter of occasional lapses, in some cases outright rebellion, then repentance ought to be a sufficient remedy for it. God forgives those who repent. But, Christians ask, if that is the case, what was the point of Jesus dying? What makes this necessary for repentance to be able to work? Sin had to be redefined as something going much

---

72. Tillich, *Systematic Theology*, vol. I, pp. 255–256.

73. Gabriel Hebert, *Fundamentalism and the Church of God* (London: SCM Press, 1957), pp. 103–116. Hebert here provides a digest version of a portion of the otherwise (still!) untranslated Swedish novel by Bo Giertz, *Stengrunnen* ("Stony Ground") which depicts the irony of pietistic elitism in traditional congregations.

deeper, a taint or curse that required more desperate measures than your or my repenting. It required the death of the Son of God. It must have, or Christ has died in vain. *So Christians inflate the doctrine of sin in order to justify the death of Christ.* This is what gave rise to the doctrine of Original Sin. What do Christians mean by this?

Some believe in *imputed guilt,* from Adam to you. This was the view of Augustine and John Cassian, Calvin and Luther. Arminians reject the imputation of Adam's sin to his progeny, but then they had best take a second look at their belief that Christ's righteousness can be imputed to believers. What's the difference? It was this realization that if imputation was bogus in the one case, it must be bogus in the other, too, that led Ethan Allen[74] to abandon Arminianism and to embrace Deism.

Arminians and other Christians think human fallenness amounts to an *irresistible tendency to sin. Environmental Sin.* This was the view of Pelagians and Ritschlians. Sooner or later you'll knuckle under to the demands and temptations of the society surrounding you. By contrast, Reinhold Niebuhr says all sin boils down to an envy based on insecurity and lack of faith in God to provide. This insecurity prompts us to try to survive and prosper by despoiling others of their needed goods. This implies the "fall" of man was a fall *into finitude.*[75]

Judaism[76] traditionally teaches a *resistible tendency to sin.* We are born with the *evil inclination,* the natural self-seeking of the child, but at the age of accountability we receive the *good inclination,* the resulting scenario resembling the cartoon in which a man listens alternatively to the urgings of a miniature devil perched on one shoul-

---

74. Ethan Allen, *Reason the Only Oracle of Man, or a Compendious System of Natural Religion* (Bennington, VT: Haswell & Russell, 1784), pp. 386–393.

75. Reinhold Niebuhr, *The Nature and Destiny of Man: A Christian Interpretation.* Gifford Lectures (New York: Scribners, 1948), pp. 178–179, 259.

76. Solomon Schechter, *Some Aspects of Rabbinic Theology* (New York: Macmillan, 1910), chapter XV., "The Evil Yetzer: The Source of Rebellion," pp. 242–263.

der, then of the tiny angel on his opposite shoulder. It is thus entirely possible to resist temptation, though too often we do not.

Total depravity describes the view of Augustine, Calvin (and, one might add, Sigmund Freud). The idea is not that everyone is as depraved as Charlie Manson all the time, but rather that there is no act, no matter how noble it seems, that is not untainted to some degree with ulterior motives of self-seeking. The distinction reminds us of the Buddhist teaching that all life is suffering, which does not mean life is an unremitting series of tortures, but rather that any joy, no matter how wonderful, must always be tinged and tainted with a shadow of the realization that it will be over too soon.

Was There a Historical Fall?

This makes less difference in Jewish theology, where sin is more of a fact of life, a characteristic of creation. Therefore it ought not surprise us that there is no official or agreed upon occasion for the Fall in Judaism. Jews tend not to read the Eden story as a Fall into sin. Some have taken Cain's murder of Abel to be the entrance point of sin. Others took the cross-breeding of the Sons of God and human females (Gen. 6:1–4) to be the opening of the flood gate for evil to corrupt human nature. In Christianity, where the Fall was a watershed drastically dividing human history before and after it, there had to be a specific moment in which it happened. The story of the Tree of Knowledge in Eden was chosen as the moment of the Fall, of disobeying God.

Because evolution sees humanity ascending from apish primitivism, not descending from a sinless pre-Fall state, some conservatives have thought it necessary to reject evolution. If humans actually *advanced* to their present state instead of falling, how can we speak of Christ restoring mankind to its lost perfection? But this need not be a problem. Irenaeus of Lyons already in the late second century had the answer. He noted that man was made in both the "image" and the "likeness" of God. The *image* was Adam in the Garden. Adam was sinless by default, untried and innocent but not yet righteous. Adam was the intended starting point. Humanity would have attained perfection in maturity but did not. Sin was a derailing of the train of human progress. We were supposed to mature into the *likeness* of God, but didn't. This ideal was realized in human flesh for the first time with Jesus Christ. And the grace of Christ enables us to get back on track, to resume our path toward the likeness of God in the New Adam, Jesus Christ. There is nothing in this that demands that humanity regressed at a particular point in time. Our "fallenness" means only that we are wandering from the true path, sheep going astray.[77]

Righteousness Like Filthy Rags

Roman Catholics and Protestant Calvinists seldom agree with Sigmund Freud, but all are at one in the conviction that our motives are never pure. But God requires purity, and, lucky for us, he himself provides that purity through the sacrifice of Christ. Calvinists say God observes a legal fiction whereby our pitiful attempts at good deeds are reckoned *as* good despite the fact that they still reek of self-deception and self-seeking ("I bet I get a big jewel in my crown for *this* one!"). But Christians and Freudians are saying something I see as quite reasonable: there is no real nobility in acts performed, deep down, from selfish motives. And that our motives are seldom completely without ulterior motives.

What I object to is the common, sweeping assumption that non-Christian good deeds *must be* somehow counterfeit, more self-interested than those done by Christians. This bigoted belief is what makes it possible for Christians to dismiss Mahatma Gandhi and the Dali Lama as damned while declaring Westboro Baptists as saved.

---

77. Augustine Hulsbosch explains this well in *God in Creation and Evolution*. Trans. Martin Versfeld (New York: Sheed and Ward, 1965).

Evangelicals swear up and down that God demands (in other words, *they* demand) correct theology, not good deeds, for salvation. To put it that bluntly admittedly sounds pretty unfair. So euphemisms abound. Why? Because they are denying human goodness is possible! No one *is* good, so no good people will be cheated out of salvation. Of course, this dismal estimate is a deduction from abstract doctrine, not an inductive inference from the evidence. So it *does* all boil down to doctrine: only those who share my creed will be saved, and *because* they share it, period. This is an example of what E.J. Carnell called "orthodoxy gone cultic."[78]

Evil-ution

Like so many other biblical ideas, that of *sin* has significantly evolved over time. It seems originally to have been, believe it or not, a nonmoral term. It did signify a transgression, but a ritual, ceremonial one. You were offending only (or primarily) God. If you steal from me, you are wronging me. But sinning is, or was, defying or blaspheming God. The first is a *wrong*, the second a *sin*. Sinning was essentially and uniquely "Godward." A prime example would be Old Testament dietary laws. If you ate a ham sandwich, you had sinned, but you had not wronged anyone (except, I guess, the pig). No one ever supposed it was *immoral* to have a shrimp cocktail. But if you did, you were flagrantly violating the categories of creation as God (i.e., the priests) had defined them. It was on this basis that the various creatures had been deemed non-kosher. You see, these dietary sins were "abominations," or more literally, "confusions," category violations. For instance, pigs were off limits because they did not qualify as legitimate "cattle." Members in good standing of this category, like cows, chewed the cud *and* had cloven hoofs. But poor Porky! His hoofs were regulation footwear, but he did not chew the

---

78. Edward John Carnell, *The Case for Orthodox Theology* (Philadelphia: Westminster Press, 1959), p. 113.

cud, in other words, partially digesting food in one stomach, breaking down the cellulose, then sending it back up for further chewing, followed by shooting the moosh down to one (or more) stomachs for yet more digestion. If you pictured Moses' stone tablets as a dinner menu, pigs would not be on it.

Or lobsters. I'm afraid you're out of luck there, too. They live in the water but don't count as fish, because genuine fish have scales and navigate by their fins. Guess what? Lobsters have a hard exoskeleton and walk on a bunch of jointed legs. So, again—off the menu. Uh, didn't God create all these critters? Why didn't he make them the way he wanted them? My theory is that originally, Israelites thought *he didn't!* I imagine that the whole kosher system derived, like so much else, from the Zoroastrianism imposed by the Persian operative Ezra. In Zoroastrian myth, it was the evil Anti-God Ahriman who created serpents, bugs, and the rest of the vermin. The righteous Ahura Mazda created all the wholesome species. Remember how Jesus granted his disciples power to tread on "snakes and scorpions and all the power of the Enemy" (Luke 10:19)? I think that's a vestige of this belief.

Even sexual infractions make sense this way. Sexual activity was made legitimate (or sanctified, if you will) by ceremonial rites of passage between categories. If not for the rituals, having sex would be as out of the question as eating pulled pork. But obviously, you have to make an exception in this case! (Interestingly, there *were* early Christian sects who embraced celibacy, even within marriage, because *nothing* could sanctify sex, which was the Original Sin.)[79]

Sex, then, required boundary-crossings: males crossing over to wed females. But within the boundaries, within the categories, no sex was allowed. This is why incest, sex within the family unit, is forbidden. Too close for comfort. This is why homosexuality was

---

79. Peter Brown, *The Body and Society: Men, Women, and Sexual Renunciation in Early Christianity.* Lectures on the History of Religions, New Series, Number 13 (New York: Columbia University Press, 1988).

forbidden. Two males? Nope; they're in the same group. Pederasty is out, because it involves crossing the adult-child boundary, and there is no ritual to make it legitimate. Same problem with bestiality. And if the Bible mentioned necrophilia, it would be outlawed for the same reason.

I think this difference between "secular" wrongs and "religious" sins explains the seeming hypocrisy of the worshipers excoriated in Isaiah chapter 1. How dare they show up in the temple in their Sunday best, piously praising Yahweh, while they were, e.g., exploiting their workers the rest of the week? My guess is that everyone had always assumed the one had nothing to do with the other! Eventually, however, things changed because of prophetic rebukes by Isaiah, Jeremiah, and others: from there on in, traditionally immoral (human-to-human) actions were considered to be equally offensive to God. Wrongs became sins. But the sacrificial system continued the old distinction, since the sins that could be expiated, washed away by the blood of an animal, were all issues of ceremonial purity. There was no sacrifice that availed for murder or adultery. You better just get out of town.

In fact, this distinction seems to underlie an important formative stage of the early Christian belief in the atonement of Christ. Sam K. Williams[80] hypothesizes that the earliest Jewish believers in Jesus believed he had been crucified but did not view it as a redeeming or atoning sacrifice. That element entered in as a way of dealing with the originally unanticipated influx of Gentiles. These Jews knew they had been sanctified via the Levitical sacrifice system. Gentiles did not have this advantage because they had never been expected or required to obey Jewish law. But once they, so to speak, applied for membership in the People of God, their ritual uncleanness immediately became a problem. How could their many years of "un-

---

80. Sam K. Williams, *Jesus' Death as Saving Event: The Background and Origin of a Concept*. Harvard Dissertations in Religion 2 (Missoula: Scholars Press, 1975).

cleanness" be dealt with? The solution was to adapt the current Hellenistic doctrine of martyrdom. In 2 Maccabees and 4 Maccabees we read of devout Jews martyred during the bloody persecution of the megalomaniac Antiochus IV Epiphanes. As they surrendered their lives, they prayed that God might regard their righteous deaths as an atonement for the sins of the people, those sins that had presumably triggered the chastisement at the hands of the pagans. (Remember: if Israel did not hold up their end of the covenant, God was no longer obliged to protect them.) The martyrs were themselves by no means guilty. After all, they were dying for the Torah!

Williams inferred that Jewish Jesus believers decided that God must have accepted Jesus' martyr death as a purifying sacrifice on behalf of the hitherto unclean Gentiles, the "nations." Christian Jews stood in no need of such purification. As faithful Jews they already had it. The historical irony was that, once Gentiles had dominated Christianity, they forgot the original meaning of the doctrine, assuming that "the nations" referred, not to non-Jews, but rather to all nations *including Jews*. You know the mischief this led to: Christians demanding that non-Christian Jews convert to Christianity. But another result was the extension of the original belief that Jesus died to (ritually) cleanse the (ritual) sins of Gentiles, reinterpreting his death as a sacrifice to absolve the *moral* transgressions of all humanity. That's quite some difference.

Real Sin

Arthur Machen (1863–1947) embodied many of the traits one might expect in a weird fiction protagonist. He was a Welsh mystic and an initiate into the Order of the Golden Dawn. Though a loyal son of the Church of England, he was also an adherent of the theory of the Grail legend as the charter of an independent, pre-Catholic Celtic Christianity. His fiction is incandescent with the witch-fire glow of the Numinous and partakes of the substance of genuine revelation.

His stories open up real depths of religious and philosophical import.

In "The Great God Pan," Machen's character Helen Vaughan is the daughter of Pan and a physician-scientist's young ward Mary. Mary was impregnated by the great god following a brain operation allowing her to pierce the mundane veil of perception and to behold Pan. The ancient Greeks believed that the sight of Pan (Greek for "all") automatically induced *panic*, holy terror, even madness. Helen eventually perishes in awful death throes in which her physiognomy and anatomy melt and mutate, manifesting the anatomy of various evolutionary stages.

In this tale we may detect a decided if implicit element of Neo-Platonism. Plotinus believed, much like the Gnostics, that all beings eventuated as emanations of the primordial One, the Good, Being in its purest form. As its substance radiated outward in wave after wave, its purity dissipated until the final stage was virtually the opposite of its source. It was matter, which was as evil as the One had been good. Matter's evil was mitigated insofar as it came to be organized according to the Platonic forms, the spiritual-rational prototypes of all physical objects. This striking vision encompassed both a kind of Pantheism, according to which the material world was a veil concealing an underlying glory of the divine, and an anti-materialistic pessimism. Insofar as the mystic attained the ecstatic glimpse of the divine, he knew his unity with God. Insofar as he might gaze upon the dark abyss of the unformed prime matter of which the world was made, he is filled with dejected, hopeless horror. It is the former which the "real sinner" (see below) seeks, the latter which Helen Vaughan reveals to her suicidal lovers and which appears onstage in the form of her deathbed dissolution into organic chaos.

A surprisingly large amount of Machen's story "The White People" is taken up with the text of a diary, and it is not exactly easy reading. It is the diary of a child who is rather more eloquent than we might expect in real life, but who nonetheless writes in a childish run-on sort of way. And the result is a distancing device unmatched in eerie effect. There is no evident artifice in it, no attempt at all to convince, and this makes it all the more convincing. "Out of the mouths of babes" (Matt. 21:16). Machen uses a brilliant variation on the "unreliable narrator" device, a gimmick designed to create an ironic distance between author and fictive narrator on the one hand, and between narrator and reader on the other. The unreliable narrator understands the action less than the reader does. But Machen's diarist knows both much *less* and much *more* than the reader does.

Machen offers another treatment of the same motif in his short tale "The Ceremony." He seems to want to say that, just as the kingdom of heaven belongs to naïve children (Mark 10:14–15), so does the hidden world generally, including its most dangerous districts. The children are, perhaps surprisingly, in especial danger because, while innocent as doves, they yet lack the serpent's wisdom (Matt. 10:16). Plus, they have not yet become blind to the alluring glimpses of a larger world as mundane adults have. Thus they are at greater risk. And the risk, even for such an innocent as the diarist in "The White People," is the commission of "real sin."

"Then the essence of sin really is . . ."

"In the taking of heaven by storm, it seems to me," said Ambrose. "It appears to me that it is simply an attempt to penetrate into another and higher sphere in a forbidden manner. You can understand why it is so rare. There are few, indeed, who wish to penetrate into other spheres, higher or lower, in ways allowed or forbidden. Men, in the mass, are amply content with life as they find it. Therefore there are few saints, and sinners (in the proper sense) are fewer still, and men of genius, who partake sometimes of each character, are rare also. Yes; on the whole, it is, perhaps, harder to be a great sinner than a great saint."

"There is something profoundly unnatural about sin? Is that what you mean?"

"Exactly. Holiness requires as great, or almost as great, an effort; but holiness works on lines that were natural once; it is an effort to recover the ecstasy that was before the Fall. But sin is an effort to gain the ecstasy and the knowledge that pertain alone to angels, and in making this effort man becomes a demon. I told you that the mere murderer is not therefore a sinner; that is true, but the sinner is sometimes a murderer. Gilles de Raiz is an instance. So you see that while the good and the evil are unnatural to man as he now is, to man the social, civilized being evil is unnatural in a much deeper sense than good. The saint endeavours to recover a gift which he has lost; the sinner tries to obtain something which was never his. In brief, he repeats the Fall."

Real sin, then, is the mirror image and the first cousin of sanctity. Both are spiritual in nature, neither is fleshly or physical. And both are heroic. Can there be heroes of sin? This is what Machen makes us ask. Not villains; of course there are villains of sin. But can there be heroes of sin? We might think of Milton's Satan, the ultimate Invictus, the captain of his soul. That he is, even though he ends in Hell. True, God has closed the best harbors to him, but he sails where he will, his craft a barge on the sulfur lake. In him the modern redefinition of Hell, proposed by C.S. Lewis, makes some sense, and it is the only case in which it does: Hell is the rewarding, the granting, of the desire of the Godless to be without God. Where is the torment in that? The common profane man, the muddled hedonist, the irreligious and unthinking, does not care one whit about the fellowship of God—and thus will not miss it! But the Miltonic Satan, the Great Satan, suffers for lack of God. Not that he wants to be with God, no, he wants to *be* God, nay, feels that he *is*. And what torments him is the injustice of the world in which he is not the deity.

Kierkegaard wrote of the knight of faith, a friend of God who, at his friend's bidding, goes questing into a howling wilderness, a chartless waste, where as much as one might desire the pointing way-markers of conventional morality and belief, one lacks them. This is the path that mystics and pioneer thinkers tread, often unable to gain a straight course. Kierkegaard's knight was the patriarch Abraham, whom God had summoned to offer his son as a sacrifice. But how could God summon a man so to smash the tablets of the divine law? Kierkegaard saw the dangerous vision of the truth: that the Word of Truth is a living word. The moment we stop our ears against its frightful voice in the name of some comforting truth enshrined from the past, we have made an idol of the old truth, and worse yet, a club with which to bludgeon the new truth to death. Old truth that bids us ignore new truth has forfeited its identity *as* the truth, and to cover up this fact it hurls the epithets "Sinner! Rebel!" against the heretic, the heeder of new truth. And thus it happens that Kierkegaard's knight of faith wears the prophetic mantle of Machen's real sinner. They are one and the same.

Put it another way: the saint is the one who does the terribly difficult thing of climbing the ladder of spiritual ascent, a ladder that is coated with the venerable gold of the religious tradition. All will praise him if he makes it to the top. The knight of faith, the real sinner, is climbing, too, only he is climbing up a Babel tower of his own building. He is seeking unauthorized access to heaven. He wants to know, like Faust, like Prometheus (who are his only gods) what secrets they are that Jehovah so jealously guards. In plain terms, he wants to know the truth that orthodoxy is afraid to know, for which it can make no room on its narrow shelf of holy and well-worn relics.

The saint takes a spiritual journey along the path prescribed and well-beaten with holy footprints. He uses the conventional doctrines and symbols to their best advantage. But the sinner, the real sinner, dares to question and even to reject those forms and names and paths. If he can leap high and far enough, he will even get, for a moment, beyond all our sheltering religious systems, all our inherited philosophies and worldviews, and he will reach the Void of outer space: the bare Suchness which no doctrine can contain and which mandates no doctrine. The Nihil, the Nothing. It is an airless heaven he has reached for a moment, but one where the stars shine all the brighter for it. He will return to earth, to walk among the familiar landmarks and familiar faces, but no longer familiar to himself. The Eden of simplicity and convention and assumption is forever barred for him, though all his contemporaries still sport blissfully within. They may see him as trapped in Hell, like Milton's Satan, but he would rather rule it than be a docile slave in heaven.

8

Predestination

When It's Least Expected, You're Elected

Traditionally Catholics and Protestants have taught that God, moved by his compassion ("grace") has provided the death of his Son as the means of salvation. If you are to accept his salvation, you must repent of your sins and "receive" Christ, for Protestants by asking him in prayer to enter your heart, for Catholics via the Eucharist. To "believe in Jesus Christ" is to trust him for your salvation. By doing this you receive the offered grace of God. It would not suffice merely to take it all for granted; you have to commit yourself to it. Saint Augustine and his latter-day disciple Martin Luther pretty much saw God's saving grace as the same thing as *predestination*, for the simple reason that human beings are dead in sin, period. We are spiritually inert and are not capable even of wanting or seeking salvation. Are we so affected by sin that we cannot seek to repent? This is the root issue, if we look at it anthropologically, from the human side. If we cannot choose salvation, God must choose it for us, and if he does, we are *predestined*. The matter may also be considered from the theological standpoint, from God's side: if he allows the freedom for sinners to repent, is his power limited? If he does not know the future before it happens, is he locked into temporality like we are?

The doctrine of predestination is the great hallmark of Calvinism, and Calvinists have espoused it in various forms. Predestination claims the support of many texts including Romans 8:29–30. What might at first appear to be "foreknowledge" texts really imply predestination, since in biblical idiom "to know" is frequently a synonym for "to choose" (e.g., Gen. 18:19, "Shall I hide from Abraham what I am about to do? After all, I have known him alone on all the earth." Also Jeremiah 1:5, "Before I formed you in the womb I knew you; before you were born, I ordained you to be a prophet to the nations." See also Gal. 1:15; Amos 3:2; Rom. 11:2). And predestination does seem to be the straightforward sense of many passages like Romans 11; 1 Thessalonians 1:4–5; 1 Corinthians 1:22–24; John 10:26–27; Acts 13:48; and Matthew 22:14. But citing proof texts is not enough if we want to understand the theological landscape. We have to survey the post-biblical history of the debate. (Besides, we may be predestined to do so!)

We begin with Pelagius, a fourth-century British monk, who taught that each individual is like Adam: innocent and theoretically capable of sinlessness. But in fact virtually everyone *does* eventually sin, corrupted by an environment full of sinners and shaped by them in inescapable ways. (Albrecht Ritschl would revive this "environmentalist" view of original sin in the nineteenth century. It is quintessentially Liberal theology). In this framework, God's "grace" simply denotes his willingness to forgive our sins and his provision of examples and exhortations for righteous living. Good works are genuinely our doing, and we are truly capable of them. We are capable of seeing the need to repent and of doing so. There is no need for divine predestination unto salvation here.

Augustine became Pelagius' opponent. He served as bishop in Hippo, North Africa, and taught that we are all born guilty of Adam's sin, having inherited both its taint and its guilt from him genetically. At least three factors led Augustine in this direction: *first*, he interpreted Romans 5:12 (which might be punctuated to mean

"Therefore as sin came into the world through one man and death through sin, and so death spread to all men *because* all sinned . . .") as meaning, "Therefore as sin came into the world through one man and death through sin, and so death spread to all men *for in him* all sinned . . ." implying all human sin was derivative from, really simultaneous with, the sin of Adam in Eden. *Second*, the logic of infant baptism: whose sin is being washed away? The baby hasn't had time to commit any! *Third*, the logic of consecrated virginity: sex must be the channel of sin; otherwise why is it better to do without it?

Again, we are dead in sin. God must cause and enable us to repent, or it isn't going to happen. Can a dead man do anything? Repentance is no exception. All subsequent good works are God's doing, the influence of his grace, not by the strength of the flesh. (Martin Luther, a centuries-later Augustinian monk, repeated all this in his book *The Bondage of the Will*). Predestination is as simple as that: God doing *for* us, *through* us, what we as moribund sinners could never do for ourselves. *Salvation by grace equals predestination*. Similarly, early twentieth-century Princeton theologian B.B. Warfield would go on to remark that predestination is identical with the very consciousness of piety itself: the refusal to credit oneself with one's own salvation or merit. (One might turn this around, however, and say that predestination is an illegitimate abstraction of that pious consciousness!)

John Cassian, a contemporary theologian and monk, mediated the debate with his compromise proposal: Semi-Pelagianism, which became official Catholic doctrine. He suggested that the sinner can indeed see the need for repentance and make a feeble, ineffective effort towards it, only to reach rapidly the end of his rope. At that point, as in later Revivalist conversion narratives, the grace of God appears out of nowhere and makes our repentance effective. What is active here is *not really predestination but rather foreknowledge*, if that. God knows who would repent, given the chance, and he makes sure they get it.

Jacob Arminius, a seventeenth-century Dutch theologian, repudiated Calvinism, a Reformation-era revival of Augustinianism. Rejecting Augustinianism as taught by Calvin a century earlier, Arminius agreed that we sinners cannot even seek to repent. God's *prevenient grace* (= "grace that goes before") must awaken us even to consider it. But then God's grace is resistible; it does not remove free choice. The choice is now newly possible, but it is not made for you by another. (Often so-called Arminians today are really Semi-Pelagians for failing to understand the key distinctions.)

The doctrine of foreknowledge (as an alternative to predestination) appeals, first, to scripture passages which assume there is no closing of options by God, that there is free will, and that God wants all to be saved. These include Acts 2:38, 40; John 3:16; 1 Timothy 2:3–4; and 2 Peter 3:9. Second, the appeal is to verses which may imply that God "chooses" those individuals whom he knows will decide to choose Christ (Rom. 8:29–30), *or that he has chosen as a broad category* those, whoever they may turn out to be, who decide for themselves to accept Christ (Eph. 1:3–4).

To this Calvinists respond that they, too, believe in free will, in addition to predestination, though only God knows how the two fit together. Thus they, too, have room for the "free will" passages. Arminians reply that the Calvinist view is not so much a holy mystery, a divine paradox, as it is simply a bad theory, full of self-contradiction, a case of wanting to have one's cake and eat it, too. Remember what Ethan Allen said: a supposed revelation should leave the truth clear and understandable, or nothing has been revealed after all!

The word *mystery*, as applied to revelation, has the same impropriety as the word supernatural. To reveal, is to make known, but for a mystery to compose any part of a revelation, is absurd; for it is the same as to reveal and not reveal at the same time; for was it revealed, it would cease to be mysterious or supernatural, but together with other parts of our knowledge would become natural.

Was a revelation, like other writings, adapted to our capacity, it might, like them be instructive to us; but a mysterious or supernatural one would not.[81]

Still, on the other hand, consider what Tillich has to say on the subject.

Whatever is essentially mysterious cannot lose its mysteriousness even when it is revealed. Otherwise something that only seemed to be mysterious would be revealed, and not that which is essentially mysterious. . . . But revelation does not dissolve the mystery into knowledge.[82]

Arminians charge that when Calvinists preach, "Whosoever will may come," they cannot mean it. Surely some are barred, having been left out of God's predestining decree. But Calvinists reply that they are speaking only to those with ears to hear. In fact, the reprobate will not want to come anyway!

Some Calvinists believed in *Infralapsarianism,* the idea that God chose certain individuals, not yet even in existence, to be saved only once Adam and Eve had fallen into sin (hence "after the Fall-ism"). If the First Couple had obeyed God, there would have been neither salvation *nor* damnation. In this schema salvation actually *depends* upon damnation. Salvation, after all, is *from* damnation, the punishment for sin. But doesn't this imply that God was surprised when Adam and Eve took a bite out of that apple? Yikes! That's no good.

Did God merely *foreknow* the Fall and the consequent lostness of all mankind and in the light of this foreseen fact predestine some to be saved from it? If so, he did not actually predestine anyone to be lost in the first place. God predestines *within* or *given* the Fall. Here predestination is contingent upon the Fall, after the Fall.

---

81. Allen, *Reason the Only Oracle of Man,* p. 207. Cf., p. 227.

82. Tillich, *Systematic Theology,* vol. I, p. 109.

But suppose God *did* know the outcome in advance. Wouldn't that mean he had already (arbitrarily) assigned salvation and damnation before anybody did anything good or bad? Well, yes! *Supralapsarians* ("before the Fall-ists") bit the bullet and decided that God actually *caused* the Fall. God actually fore-ordained the Fall itself as a means of salvation. He has in mind a nifty plan of salvation, but he needs some people to be lost first! So he sets up a trial in Eden to see if Adam will have the fortitude to obey him and resist Satan's temptation.

The big problem with all this is that it makes God into a devil, creating the majority of his human pets only to fuel the ovens of hell. Calvinist theologian Francis Turretin tried his best to mitigate this horror by explaining that God, er, ah, did not exactly *force* Adam and Eve to sin. No, he, uh, only "pulled the plug" on his grace which had hitherto upheld Ozzie and Harriet in their innocence. What a dirty trick! I can't help thinking of a comic book story[83] in which the Mighty Thor was about to defeat his rival Hercules in even combat—until an irate Odin suddenly cut Thor's power in half! Any theology that seriously suggests such things is really just superstition, teaching its flock to kowtow shivering before a demonic tyrant.

At the Synod of Dort, Calvinist theologians took it a surprising step further: they concluded that predestination means everything *had* to happen as it did. And this in turn implies that God himself had no free will! God's decrees, they said, proceed directly from his eternal and immutable nature. This is virtually the same as Spinoza's pantheism: every event is simply the logical unfolding of the divine Nature. This is only one example; we will see other aspects of Christian theism that seem to point in the direction of Eastern thought. That's not necessarily bad, but it does tend to undermine Christian theology, to hint that that theology may not really be what Christians *think* it is!

---

83. Stan Lee, Jack Kirby, and Vince Colletta, "Clash of the Titans" in *Thor Annual* # 1 (New York: Marvel Comics; 1965).

Augustine's views on predestination weren't static. At first he believed in *single predestination*. He figured that God picked out certain individuals to be saved but just left everybody else to their fate. He didn't actually *choose* anybody to fry in hell; he just didn't bother to *save* them from it. But the more he thought about it, the more it seemed to him that he was drawing a false distinction. Okay, then: God assigned some to salvation, others to damnation. And he made this choice prior to and independent of anything they *might* do, or that God knew in advance that they *would* do. This is what Calvinists call "unconditional election."

God must choose both fates. This means there is *double predestination*: God chooses both the elect for salvation and the reprobate for damnation. Calvin pursued the same theological evolution, following Augustine inevitably step by step down the same path of logic.

But you know all about the law of unintended consequences, right? This version of predestination ("unconditional election") allowed for the daunting possibility that, even though you might repent and believe as sincerely as you know how, you might still be on God's naughty list! "Grace" becomes mere arbitrariness.

John Calvin did not see the problem. As far as he was concerned, the doctrine of predestination should be a great comfort to the Christian, since he needn't worry whether he were a good enough Christian because he knew his salvation depended on God's election, not on the Christian's performance. Augustine had not been under any such delusion. He would have considered such comforting confidence to be rank presumption.

But later, the Puritans saw what Augustine saw and what Calvin did not: if God's choice is inscrutable and unconditional, then you can never know for sure whether you're "saved" or not! "Well, I sure do *want* to serve Christ with all my heart. Doesn't that mean I'm *in*?" Whoa! Slow down there, pal! You remember that Sunday School teacher who seemed so pious—until he ran off with the choir director? He probably thought *he* was a good Christian, too, until his true colors emerged, surprising even himself. Hoo boy! This, too, is superstition of a sort, just like Plutarch said, "The atheist believes there is no God; the superstitious man believes there is but wishes there weren't."

The Hopkinsian faction of Calvinism in the eighteenth century decided to make the best of it. They resolved to love God even if their devotion *were* somehow counterfeit. They would be happy, if it came to that, to be damned and suffer in hell for the glory of God![84] Now we're talking about insanity.

The Puritans dealt with the problem of never being able to be sure you were one of the elect, by looking for "signs of election." Economic success was one of these. Another was to have a conversion experience, a dateable "experience of grace." If you weren't able to point to one, but you were a believer nonetheless, you'd be permitted to attend church, but you couldn't take communion. Solomon Stoddard came up with this "halfway covenant." Though the Methodist revivalists and Free Will Baptist evangelists rejected predestination, they still affirmed the need for a definite, *felt* "born again" experience, a "heart-warming" experience as John Wesley called it. An abundance of surviving diaries, letters, and clinical reports from the nineteenth century reveal an epidemic of crippling anxiety, depression, even suicides, among Protestant pietists who just could not produce such an experience no matter how hard they tried.[85]

These stories of frustrated seekers could be taken to reinforce the idea that you might be a sincere believer and yet find yourself shut out of God's grace. But there is also a subgenre of conversion tales in which seekers first give up in despair, only to receive the blessing

---

84. "The sovereignty of God and the negation of man both reach a terrifying climax here in a vision of the damned themselves joining in the glorification of that same God who has sentenced them to damnation." Berger, *Sacred Canopy*, p. 75.

85. Julius H. Rubin, *Religious Melancholy and Protestant Experience in America* (New York: Oxford University Press, 1994).

after all! Surprised by joy! These stories circulate in order to give new hope to the "sick souls."[86] But it's a mind game you cannot win. That's because you *can't* despair of a successful experience of grace, since you now know the happy ending of the story. So you cannot do what the people in the old stories did. Your mourner's bench despair must be a sham.

86. William James, *The Varieties of Religious Experience: A Study in Human Nature*. Gifford Lectures 1901–1902 (New York: A Mentor Book/New American Library, 1958), Lectures VI and VII, "The Sick Soul," pp. 112–139.

9

The Atoning Death of Christ
Cross Purposes

The usual excuse for believing in damnation is that God must be *just* as well as *merciful*, or he will be cheating. He would be sweeping sin under the rug. No, he has to deal with sin, make sure it is paid for. He is no bleeding-heart liberal who empties the prisons into the streets from an exaggerated sense of compassion.

What do you think made the atoning death of Jesus Christ needful? His Father had to take the penalty for sin out of *someone*'s hide. And that someone had to belong to the group that owed the debt. And yet it must be an individual who had not himself contributed to the debt. Theoretically, perhaps, God himself could have paid the debt (with his eternal life), but then again, he does not owe it. Mankind does owe it but cannot pay it except by total damnation. The solution (and it is a marvelously clever one, devised by Anselm in the eleventh century): God becomes a member of mankind via the Incarnation. He bears the sin of his kind, though he himself is not personally implicated. Mankind is henceforth off the hook, though one must still make a personal decision to embrace that atonement.

But the idea of "Christ dying for our sins" does not make any sense. C.S. Lewis[87] offers us a basic faith which is content just to believe that the Cross of Jesus saves while requiring no particular explanation of *how* it saves. Specific atonement doctrines are secondary, he says. It's nothing to divide the church over. But, as too often, Lewis is too facile. There is a deeper problem than Christian factionalism here. Why are there so many different atonement doctrines? Because all of them are vitiated by severe problems. If anyone of them made sense, wouldn't everyone be happy to agree on it? Let's go over a few of the major ones.

Does it clear things up to consider Jesus' death an *expiation*? That would mean his spilled blood cleansed us of sin in the same way the blood of a sacrificial animal supposedly washed away the sin of the ancient Israelite. The animal sacrifice idea is itself no more intelligible than the cross business: it is an attempt to explain one puzzle by means of another.

Is it any better to say Jesus' death is a *penal substitution*, letting John Wayne Gacy go free if the Pope were willing to take his place in the gas chamber? Hardly! What sort of justice is this? If you piously believe this one, maybe you never notice the problem, any more than Gacy would question the propriety of the substitution as he packed his bags and left Death Row behind. Don't look a gift horse in the mouth. But how can it have been "just" to allow an innocent man to take the rap for the crimes of another, even if the innocent party agreed? I think the whole thing is based on a failure of ancient law to distinguish between torts and crimes, as if all you had to do for any offense was to buy your way out of it. And if someone else put up the money in your place, you were free to go. Forget about mercy—this isn't even justice!

---

87. Lewis, *Mere Christianity*, p. 57: "The central Christian belief is that Christ's death has somehow put us right with God and given us a new start. Theories as to how it does this are another matter. A good many theories have been held as to how it works; all Christians are agreed on is that it does work."

Universalist theologian Hosea Ballou,[88] much influenced by Deist Ethan Allen, just could not jettison this doctrine fast enough. Ballou invited us to imagine some guy trying to assassinate the President and failing. He is captured and sentenced to death. But, lo and behold, the President himself asks for his would-be killer to receive clemency, *offering to be hanged in the attempted assassin's place!* Would we, Ballou asks, think any of this to be appropriate, much less just, for a single moment? No freakin' way! It would be morally twisted nonsense!

How about Athanasius' doctrine that God had to live a truly mortal life (including a death) in order to infuse mortals with his own immortality? Sounds good, but besides the questionable business of picturing immortality like some kind of a permeating grease, this one runs aground on the rock (as Thomas J.J. Altizer[89] noted) that no mortal dies for only a couple of days. This theory would work better if there were no resurrection in the story. Now *that* would be a real death. As we read it in the gospels, we have a docetic charade.

Gregory of Nyssa formulated a theory whereby Jesus' death was a scam to outwit a kidnapper named Satan, who held the whole (sinful) human race hostage. God the Father knew how much Satan would love to add Jesus' immortal soul to his collection (think of Mr. Scratch with his collection of moths in *The Devil and Daniel Webster*), so he offered to barter Jesus' death for the return of the hostages. Satan fell for it, poor dope, not realizing that he couldn't keep a good man down. Jesus rose from the dead, escaping Satan's clutches, and left the poor devil holding the bag. The crass mythological character of this hardly requires comment.

Peter Abelard tried to short-circuit all these theories (and more like them) by saying simply that Jesus' death saves us by demonstrating the love of God. But this is exceedingly lame. How does the mere

---

88. Ballou, *Treatise on Atonement*, pp. 79–80.

89. Thomas J.J. Altizer, *The Descent into Hell: A Study of the Radical Reversal of Christian Consciousness* (Philadelphia: Lippincott, 1970).

fact of a death, implicitly one that would otherwise have been avoidable, show love? The death could show love only if dying were the only way to save us. If I jumped in front of a speeding car to knock you out of its path, and I died, then my death would indeed show my love for you. But if you are not in any danger and I say, "Watch this!" and jump in front of a car, I'm just crazy.

Little better is Donald M. Baillie's Neo-Orthodox classic *God Was in Christ*,[90] where he argued that the sufferings of the incarnate Christ boil down to the sentimental truism that there is no forgiveness without a painful cost. The father of the Prodigal Son had to blink back the tears of painful memory in order to accept his wayward son back, is that it? On the contrary, the Prodigal's father hasn't a thought about the past. He runs to embrace his son joyously. Just the way Jesus (before the Last Supper, anyway) says God forgives sinners—freely! As Harnack[91] pointedly asked in his *What Is Christianity?*, are we to imagine that Jesus went about preaching God's free forgiveness to the repentant, only to change the terms of forgiveness as of the crucifixion? Now it seems it took a cross, and that you must believe in a cross. The change must have come as a way of making sense of the death of Jesus: if he had to die for sins, then we must have needed him to die! From "effect" to "cause."

And thus the plethora of bizarre atonement theories. Old Washington Gladden[92] hit the nail on the head: "The figures used by these theologians are so grotesque that it is difficult to quote them without incurring the charge of treating sacred themes with levity." Again he says,

---

90. Donald M. Baillie, *God Was in Christ: An Essay on Incarnation and Atonement* (New York: Scribners, 1948), pp. 201–202.

91. Adolf Harnack, *What Is Christianity?* Trans. Thomas Bailey Saunders. Harper Torchbooks (New York: Harper & Row, 1957), p. 143.

92. Washington Gladden, *How Much Is Left of the Old Doctrines? A Book for the People* (Boston and New York: Houghton, Mifflin and Company, 1899), p. 178.

It is easy to see why these theories have either perished or become moribund. It is because they are morally defective. They ascribe to God traits of character and principles of conduct which are repugnant to our sense of right. It is because men are compelled to believe that the Judge of all the earth will do right, that they cannot believe these theories.[93]

To these morally reprehensible atonement doctrines one must add any doctrine of the cross that leads to the conclusion that people will be damned to eternal torture for not believing in it.

Bultmann recognized the difficulties with rationally explaining the atonement and he saw them as prime evidence for his claim that mythology taken literally contradicts the point the myth itself seeks to make. For example, myth says that God lives up in heaven. In philosophical language, the point would seem to be the transcendence of God. But the heaven business, taken literally, implies that God is simply far removed in space,[94] as if he were an alien being living on another planet (which is just what some literal-minded eccentrics have made him! Remember all those books with titles like *God Drives a Flying Saucer!*).[95] So the point is reversed and negated if you pause for a second to notice and then to insist on a literal application.

The same goes for the atonement. Bultmann says the point of the myth that a god should come down from heaven, assume human flesh, and die for the sins of mortals, is to say that God forgives by

93. Washington Gladden, *Present Day Theology* (Columbus, OH: McClelland and Company, 1912), p. 162.

94. Rudolf Bultmann, "New Testament and Mythology" in Hans Werner Bartsch, ed., *Kerygma and Myth: A Theological Debate*. Trans. Reginald H. Fuller. Harper Torchbooks (New York: Harper & Row, 1961), p. 10, fn 2: "Mythology is the use of imagery to express the other worldly in terms of this world and the divine in terms of human life, the other side in terms of this side. For instance, divine transcendence is expressed as spatial distance."

95. R.L. Dione, *God Drives a Flying Saucer* (New York: Bantam Books, 1973).

grace, not by any human effort. It's all from his side, not ours. But all these atonement theories assume that there was a literal transaction of some sort on the cross the day Jesus died. And the implications, as we have seen, are absurd. It's like asking how the Pharisees came to be noticing that Jesus dined with publicans and sinners unless they did, too (Mark 2:15–17). How else would they have known? Or why would the woman sweep her whole house by lamplight searching for a lost drachma until she found it—and then blow the money by inviting her neighbors over for a party to celebrate it (Luke 15:8–10) !? You're missing the point.

In the same way, from Bultmann's perspective, the ugly scenario of a supposedly loving Father condemning his innocent but obedient Son to crucifixion is an unintended consequence of the powerful myth of the atoning cross. You're not supposed to take the details literally. Any more than you would ask if the prince and the princess really lived happily ever after—with no quarrels? No money problems?

I once saw the ultimate example of someone following out the atonement myth to its most grotesque extreme. It was an evangelistic tract in which a kid's dad punished him for swearing by making the kid whip his dad with his own belt, insisting on it even when his shocked son quails at the prospect of lacerating his beloved dad. One can hardly imagine Ward and the Beaver in such a kinky scenario. But you have to give the writer credit for being consistently literal. He had followed out the premise of the innocent suffering on behalf of the sinner to its bitter end. And in the process he had proven that this was exactly the wrong way to go!

I guess Bultmann was right. It seemed to work pretty well when Billy Graham preached forgiveness through the cross without digressing into theology lessons about how this might work. The power of the myth shines through the myth only when it is not obscured, ironically, with rationalistic attempts to make it make sense (which it doesn't anyway!).

Or, on second thought, did it work simply because Billy was not letting his buyers get a close look at the product he was selling them? If they thought it all the way through, would they still have thought it sounded viable? Maybe Bultmann's is really little more than an attempt to cover up the problems with a band-aid. Is his non-theology of the cross any better than those desperate chauvinists who admit Paul's specific arguments against women's equality are fallacious but that we have to accept his conclusion anyway? Accept the conclusion after kicking away all the supports for it?

And has Bultmann forgotten that the whole doctrine of the saving cross arose in the first place as a way to rationalize the scandal of why Jesus died on a criminal's cross? There's the same rationalizing process he laments.

Meet the New Gospel, Same as the Old Gospel

Catholics and conservative Protestants say, "Look, God *is* merciful! He's given you a way *out* of Hell! All it entails is admitting you're a sinner, believing in Jesus, etc." Leaving aside the huge matter of whether there is sufficient reason to believe in Jesus, and the injustice of requiring us to believe without sufficient evidence, it seems to me that as long as we are still required to do something, and we are told that, if we don't, we are morally culpable, then nothing fundamental has changed because of the death of Christ. It may be a different set of hoops one is required to jump through, but I thought grace was about no longer having to jump!

It is just such vitiating self-contradictions and logical convolutions that make many of us decide that Christian theology is not so much false as absurd. And for Christians to insist that we believe it by faith, even though there is nothing coherent to believe, is just like the Thought Police officer O'Brien in George Orwell's *1984*: he insists we believe there are three lights when we know there are only two. Otherwise we will not be released from torture. How revealing, then, that theologians tell us that "faith is a gift," or that it is predestined. Aren't they admitting that they wouldn't believe it either if not for the divine hypnosis of "grace"?

10

The Resurrection

The Mummy's Tomb

In the New Testament writings, the theological meaning of the resurrection of Jesus is treated in various ways, though they are not so
very different as to count as contradictions. Luke and Acts are a bit
different from the rest, but this is mainly because of a significant
difference in their respective treatments of the *death* of Christ. Luke
seems to shun the understanding of the crucifixion as an atonement,
viewing it instead as a prophetically predicted martyrdom (Luke
24:25–26; Acts 2:22–2). This is surprising since Jews of the time
viewed martyrdom as an atonement for the sins of the persecuted
people (2 Macc. 7:1–42; 4 Macc. 6:27–29; 17:20–22). Salvation, for
Luke, comes through the name of Jesus, i.e., baptism in that name
(Acts 2:38). The importance of Jesus' death is that, since the Messiah
was predicted to suffer and die, Jesus could not be the true Messiah
had he not gone to the cross. Resurrection, then, was simply God's
vindication of Jesus (Acts 2:36), reversing what Paul called "the scandal of the cross" (1 Cor. 1:33).

The Pauline Epistles speak of Jesus' resurrection as instrumental
for salvation. One must believe, not only in Jesus, even a crucified Jesus, but specifically in the resurrection of Jesus (Rom. 10:9). Not only

the death but also the resurrection occurred for the sake of our salvation (Rom. 4:25). This is probably why he insists that, if Jesus had not risen there would be no hope for life beyond death (1 Cor. 15:19; 1 Thes. 4:13–14). Jesus' resurrection demonstrates that it is possible to "bounce back" from death. In fact, Jesus' resurrection should be understood as the "leading edge" of the general resurrection of believers at the soon-coming end of the age. The end had to be near since the process had begun! (Of course it didn't quite work out that way.)

At least as important was the resurrection of Jesus as his enthronement at the right hand of God where he reigns invisibly. Eric Franklin[96] suggested that this aspect of the resurrection belief was a secondary development in early Christian theology. As he sees it, the enthronement of Jesus was an attempt to adjust to the delay of the Parousia, the triumphant return of Jesus as the messianic ruler. It hadn't happened "on schedule," and Christians were enduring persecution and "kept watching the sky,"[97] hoping for deliverance, but in vain. "Don't give up!" Luke says; things may look bad now, but remember, the Lord Jesus is in charge, and he knows what he's doing. Though Franklin himself does not draw the parallel, I cannot help comparing his scenario with that of Jehovah's Witnesses after their 1918 deadline for the Second Coming fell through: "Don't worry, folks—he *did* assume his reign, but, er, in*vi*sibly, up in heaven, not here on earth!" Yeah, *that*'s the ticket!

It Takes a Miracle—or Does it?

Modern New Testament scholars no longer take for granted that the Easter narratives are history at all. Why *should* they be? The gospel tales are so much like similar apotheosis narratives of Hercules, Ro-

---

96. Eric Franklin, *Christ the Lord: A Study in the Purpose and Theology of Luke-Acts* (Philadelphia: Westminster Press, 1975).

97. As reporter Ned Scott urges his listeners at the end of *The Thing from Another World*.

mulus, Apollonius, Empedocles and others that the burden of proof is on anyone who would insist that, in the single case of Jesus, "myth became fact." And such is manifestly a theological judgment, not a historical verdict. But the important thing to see is that the chain of "events" leading up to the epiphany of the Risen One is equally legendary: mere stage setting for the Big "Event." Scholars do not suppose that, say, the Joseph of Arimathea story, or that of the women visiting the tomb, is history, and that the only thing that requires special explanation is why the tomb was empty. Why should they/ we? Apologists long ago lost the game by misidentifying the kind of narrative we are dealing with in Mark 15–16, Matthew 27–28, Luke 23–24, and John 19–21. It is pious fiction. But for the sake of argument, let us play the apologists' game, treating the main events of the story as factual. I do not think one has to reach very far to see an altogether natural explanation for the supposed resurrection.

Apologists think they can refute the *Scheintod* (seeming death) theory by proof texting D.F. Strauss who derided the notion that a crucified but living Jesus, broken and bleeding, might have staggered into the midst of his disciples posing as the mighty victor over death.

> It is impossible that a being who had stolen half-dead out of the sepulchre, who crept about weak and ill, wanting medical treatment, who required bandaging, strengthening and indulgence, and who still at last yielded to his sufferings, could have given to the disciples the impression that he was a Conqueror over death and the grave, the Prince of Life, an impression which lay at the bottom of their future ministry. Such a resuscitation could only have weakened the impression which he had made upon them in life and in death, at the most could only have given it an elegiac voice, but could by no possibility have changed their sorrow into enthusiasm, have elevated their reverence into worship.[98]

---

98. David Friedrich Strauss, *The Life of Jesus for the People*. Theological Translation Fund Library (London: Williams & Norgate, 2nd ed., 1879), vol. I, p. 412.

It *is* a slightly comical scene, but it is not a scene required or implied by the *Scheintod* Theory. All the theory (or the Swoon theory as it is also called) entails is a Jesus who, in the providence of his Father, cheated death, and whose beloved Sonship was thereby confirmed the more securely. The ensuing doting of his relieved disciples upon the recuperating savior would only have fed the instinct to worship him. All one has to surmise is that he waited a while, till he was better and stronger, to make grandiose pronouncements. But let's back up. What suggests the Swoon Theory? I think the texts themselves suggest it, so strongly in fact, that it does seem to me that the *Scheintod* model was the actual teaching of the gospels at some earlier stage. It has since been redacted out in the course of the evolution of early Christian belief.

First, there is Jesus' prayer in the Garden of Gethsemane in Mark 14:35–36: "And going a little farther, he fell on the ground and prayed that, if it were possible, the hour might pass from him. And he said, 'Abba, Father, all things are possible to thee; remove this cup from me; yet not what I will, but what thou wilt.'" It reads most naturally to me as if Mark intended this supplication to receive an answer, despite initial appearances: "In the days of his flesh, Jesus offered up prayers and supplications, with loud cries and tears, to him who was able to save him from death, and he was heard for his godly fear" (Heb. 5:7). And if that is not a reading of the Gethsemane prayer that envisions God delivering Jesus as he asked, I don't know what the words mean. In short, the text seems to anticipate that it is Jesus' willingness to go the way of sacrifice that atoned for Israel, just as, in much Rabbinic thinking, it was the willingness of Isaac to die, and not any eventuality of his actual death, that expiated future Israel's sins.

Second, there is the surprise of Pontius Pilate that Jesus had expired so quickly, implying that maybe he *hadn't*.

Joseph of Arimathea, a respected member of the council, who was also himself looking for the kingdom of God, took courage and went to Pilate, and asked for the body of Jesus. And Pilate wondered if he were already dead; and summoning the centurion, he asked him whether he was already dead. And when he learned from the centurion that he was dead, he granted the body to Joseph. (Mark 15:43–45).

Surely this odd fact, Jesus' as-yet unexplained premature death, is the first shoe dropping. We are left expecting the second: he is not dead, but only drugged. Indeed, the attention and build-up devoted to giving Jesus a drink is surprising if there will not prove to have been some pay-off.

Likewise, the mockery of the Sanhedrinists (15.34: "Let the Christ, the King of Israel, come down now from the cross, that we may see and believe!") is delightful irony indeed if Jesus is in fact going to demonstrate his divine Sonship by coming down from the cross alive. Is this all coincidence? Only a flat, blindfolded reading of Mark says so.

I am not the first to note the surprising parallel between Mark 15:43–45 and the account of Josephus bar-Matthias the historian of how he recognized a former ally on the cross and prevailed upon Titus to have him taken down, saving his life.

I saw many captives crucified, and remembered three of them as my former acquaintances. I was very sorry at this in my mind, and went with tears in my eyes to Titus, and told him of them; so he immediately commanded them to be taken down, and to have the greatest care taken of them, in order to their recovery; yet two of them died under the physician's hands, while the third recovered. (*Life* 75, William Whiston trans.)

One might plausibly argue that Mark's story is actually borrowed from Josephus ("Joseph of Arimathea" = "Joseph bar-Matthias"). But if not, the Josephus story at least parallels the Markan version as I am suggesting we understand it.

Third, speaking of Joseph of Arimathea, why does Matthew tell us that he was rich (27:57)? It can hardly be intended as one more fulfillment of prophecy, this time (as one might suggest but Matthew does not say) Isaiah 53:9, "And they made his grave with the wicked and with a rich man in his death." For one thing, Matthew always calls attention to prophetic fulfillments (see the nativity story, etc.: Matt. 1:22; 2:517, 23; 4:14). For another, he can hardly have considered Joseph a wicked man and indeed says just the opposite (Matt. 27:57). So what is the detail doing there? I believe it is meant to provide narrative motivation for grave robbers breaking into the newly sealed opulent tomb in which only the bruised and beaten scarecrow Jesus awaits, contrary to their expectations. Robbers, as they do in ancient novels of this period (Chariton's *Chaereas and Callirhoe*, Xenophon's *Ephesian Tale*), break into newly sealed, opulent tombs hoping to find rich funerary tokens, a la the Pharaohs, but find only a victim of unwitting premature burial returning to consciousness.

Fourth, Luke's reunion scene in which Jesus demonstrates his corporeality (Luke 24:36–43) may naturally be read as a striking parallel to that of Apollonius of Tyana when he reappears across the Mediterranean to greet his disciples who have assumed him executed by the Roman tyrant Domitian and now think him a ghost.

> Damis groaned out loud, and said something like, "Gods above, will we ever see our good, noble comrade?"
>
> Apollonius, who was now standing at the entrance of the grotto, heard this and said, "You will, in fact you already have."
>
> "Alive?" asked Demetrius. "But if dead, we have never stopped weeping for you."
>
> Apollonius stretched out his hand, and said, "Take hold of me. If I elude you, I am a ghost come back from Persephone's domain, like

the ghosts which the gods below reveal to men when mourning makes them too despondent. But if I stay when you grasp me, persuade Damis, too, that I am alive and have not lost my body." (Philostratus, *Life of Apollonius of Tyana* 8:12, C.P. Jones trans.)

The point of the Apollonius scene (and I believe the point of the Lukan) is pointedly not that the hero has died and returned in some manner from the dead, but rather that he has *escaped* death. He did not die. In both cases we are told the disciples first imagined they were seeing their master's ghost, only to be assured of his living corporeality. He has not died after all. Why does John change the story, so that the point is now not only corporeality but tangible mortal wounds? Precisely to close off this possibility of understanding Jesus as having eluded death. It is only in John 20 that we ever read that Jesus was nailed to the cross instead, say, of being merely tied to it, as was often done. It is only in John 19:34–37 and 20:25, 27 that we read of a fatal stab wound through the ribs. John has added these "details" to make sure the reader knows Jesus was really dead, something he must have had to do since many did not think so. This is also likely why he laughs off the speculation of Jesus' enemies that he might be planning to leave Palestine to travel among the Diaspora (John 7:35); that's what he must have done if he survived crucifixion, fleeing Palestine as Aristotle did Athens when trouble reared its head, "lest Athens sin twice against philosophy."

It is quite common for the followers of slain heroes and leaders to claim their man did not die but only went into hiding, so the fact that some early Christians told the story of Jesus this way is hardly proof that he did actually survive crucifixion. But my point is that, in view of all these factors in the text, which otherwise are all pointless red herrings in the narrative, it is by no means some expedient of desperation to suggest that Jesus was drugged on the cross, taken down prematurely, and survived at least for a while. This is only to follow the lead of the texts themselves, as I see it.

The apologetical trump card against this possibility is that the Roman guards at the tomb would have constituted quite a barrier for an ailing, wounded Jesus. How could he have gotten by them? Again, I will not belabor the obvious: only Matthew mentions such guards, an impossibility if there was such a detachment. But let's assume Matthew is right and that the other evangelists somehow dismissed this portion of the story as an unimportant trifle unworthy of mention. In that case, perhaps it was these soldiers who took the elementary precaution of checking the contents of the tomb before sealing it. There had been, after all, something of an interval between Joseph burying Jesus and the Sanhedrin petitioning Pilate for the guards. They must have checked. And if Jesus were reviving, there is just no reason to believe they would have locked him in alive! Maybe they would have fled as Mark's women did, victim to superstitious fear. Or maybe they would have helped the "broken man" to safety.

As I read John's Easter account in 20:11–15, I do not need to impose some sort of Jesus-hating skepticism in order to "escape" the implications of the text. No, I find myself reading along reverently, appreciating the sense of numinous "ozone" in this wonderful story, and I am suddenly taken aback when Mary Magdalene finds no one in the tomb: O God! Is there to be no end to the horrors of this weekend? What *now*? She asks a man standing nearby, apparently the caretaker of the mausoleum grounds, if he has already transferred the corpse somewhere else. She does not wonder what may have happened to it. It's pretty obvious. As we, too, have been told in 19:41–42, "Now in the place where he was crucified there was a garden, and in the garden a new tomb where no one had ever been laid. So because of the Jewish day of Preparation, as the tomb was close at hand, they laid Jesus there." Jesus' remains had been deposited in this nearby tomb only as an emergency measure since time was running out. It was not meant to stay there. Mary is only concerned that she may be unable to find out the final resting place. This is not some weird speculation.

This is the scenario laid out by the gospel itself. And though the evangelist (obviously) goes on to supply an alternate explanation, that of faith in the resurrection of Jesus, the text itself has already supplied a purely natural explanation for an empty tomb as well as the implication that Christians might not have been privy (or ever become privy) to Jesus' final resting place. John himself tells us that the prima facie explanation was a simple relocation of a corpse hastily stashed there for the moment. Maybe this is what happened. Bingo: Jesus is buried, the empty tomb is discovered, and it is too late to find out where the body has been taken, perhaps because the disciples did not know of the role of Joseph of Arimathea and Nicodemus. Maybe the custodian Mary asked had replaced the man who had approved the removal of the body on an earlier shift, and he simply did not know what to tell her. ("No ma'am, I don't know where he is; sorry.") There is no bafflement here that would have us welcoming supernatural miracles as a better explanation, is there?

If we were not so familiar with the text, it would strike us as quite ludicrous to think one must draw the inference from the empty tomb that Jesus must therefore have been raised from the dead, fully as absurd as the scene from *Monty Python's Life of Brian* in which Brian's followers momentarily lose track of him in the middle of a crowd and jump to the conclusion, "He's been taken up!" "No, there he is!"

Elvis Sightings

At first glance, the idea that the Risen Lord was, ah, somebody else, maybe some other savior, or somebody impersonating Jesus, seems silly. Mistaken identity? You've got to be kidding. But the gospels themselves introduce this suspicion, not that someone was impersonating the slain Jesus, but that his mourning disciples, ill-inclined to let go of him, grasped at the straw that some unknown individual they had met shortly after the crucifixion must actually have been

Jesus, alive again. The disciples on the way to Emmaus (Luke 24:13–35) talk with the man for hours, and only as he vanishes does it occur to them it was their old master. The eleven disciples, even as they are issued their marching orders, wonder if it is really he (Matt. 28:17, "but they [not "some"] doubted"). Mary at the tomb does not recognize Jesus, either (John 20:14). The disillusioned disciples, readjusting to a mundane career, see Jesus on shore but they do not recognize him (John 21:4). Let us give apologists the benefit of the doubt and consider the implications if these gospel stories were, as they insist, genuine accounts of Easter encounters. All this non-recognition business, which we should never have expected, inevitably invites the suspicion that the Easter encounters were actually sightings of, encounters with, figures only later identified with Jesus, and that as a means of escaping grief and despair. "Realizing" it in retrospect was not as good as realizing it at the time, but then there was an advantage, too: it could not be debunked.

Mark (6:14; 8:28) supplies a striking precedent when he tells us (twice, no less) that many people believed they were seeing or hearing about a resurrected John the Baptist, even though Mark claims to know better: it was a case of mistaken identity, since the figure was actually Jesus. It is no great stretch to wonder if the same thing happened in the case of Jesus.

Let us imagine ourselves among the apostolic community in those early days. We hear reports from several of the brethren that they have seen the slain Jesus alive again. Naturally our eyes widen; our ears perk up. And, like Thomas, we ask, "Are you sure? Tell me about it!" One tells us, "Of course I didn't realize it was Jesus at the time. It only dawned on me later." Another says, "It didn't really look like him, I admit, but later on I realized it must have been Jesus." And so on. I submit to you that we would be well justified to wonder what might have happened, and not to be convinced that our friends had actually seen Jesus. Their own testimonies would have created doubt instead of faith.

The Descent into Hell

There is another problem with the doctrine of Jesus' resurrection, far worse than the inability to prove that it happened. As many skeptics have long pointed out, the resurrection would seem to negate the importance of the saving death of Jesus. Of the New Testament writers, only Luke seems even possibly to have been aware of this, and it would make a lot of sense for this to have been the reason for Luke's eliminating the element of atonement from his mentions of Jesus' death. If we are to view Jesus' death as an eternal sacrifice made to absolve the human race of sins, Jesus' return to life on the third day must severely lessen the gravity of that "sacrifice." Jesus, in that case, suffered (admittedly awfully) for some six hours, which, even according to the gospel narrative, was abnormally short (Mark 15:44–45). Forgive me for saying so, but this pales to insignificance next to the suffering of tortured Jews in the Nazi concentration camps. Jesus' death would be the envy of an actual martyr! His crucifixion hardly even *counts* as a real death, any more than some Near Death Experience on the operating table. These are hard words, I know.

I say Luke avoids the problem, and that's because, for him, the crucifixion of Jesus was but a temporary setback, the darkness before the dawn, a failed attempt to get rid of him reversed dramatically by God. But Christian theology cannot afford to deal with the problem. On one level, an adjustment could be made: just drop the atonement business and default to the Lukan soteriology whereby one needs simply to affirm faith in Jesus and be baptized calling on his name. But you know that's never going to happen. There's been way too much maudlin talk about being washed in the blood of the Lamb to backtrack on it now. Radical theologian Thomas J.J. Altizer proposed an alternative way of conceiving Jesus' death as a saving event, though it entails a very non-traditional understanding of salvation. Altizer bids us to embrace the Death of God, the gospel of Christian Atheism. At the cross, Altizer proclaims, the Transcendant

God kenotically (Phil. 2:6–11) poured himself out, the Sacred into the Profane, with the result that, a la Buddhism, Nirvana must be discerned within Samsara. As in Spinoza's pantheism, the Divine is concealed, yet simultaneously revealed. Christ's incarnation continues because his death endures, too. He never reversed the Cross but dwells now as a witch-fire radiance, a trace, of the Holy. For example, one seeks Christ in the least of his suffering brethren. This gospel would seem the exact opposite of the charismatic triumphalism condemned in 2 Corinthians and on garish display with Porsche-driving TV evangelists but also in the finery of cardinals and popes. An appropriate spirituality for the Secular City[99] would be that demonstrated in Malcolm Boyd's once-popular collection of on-the-spot prayers, *Are You Running with Me, Jesus?*

Incidentally, Altizer's gospel would qualify as another example of an apt demythologing of an archaic Christian doctrine, the picturesque account of Jesus descending into the lava-spewing caverns of the subterranean Hell to liberate the souls of the righteous held captive there since Adam, awaiting their Savior. In the apocryphal Gospel of Nicodemus we witness the panic of Satan and Beelzebub as their security cameras reveal the approach of Jesus to trash the place and set the captives free.

Where does this outrageously mythic scenario come from? It may have grown up from three New Testament passages: Matthew 27:52–53, 1 Peter 3:18–20, and Ephesians 4:8–10. In the first, coincident with Jesus' death, a group of dead saints come to life again and visit Jerusalem. In the second, it seems that, as of the resurrection, Jesus visited Tartarus to preach good news to spirits imprisoned there. The third is taken to describe Jesus' ascension, taking a mysterious company with him. These fragments have been patched together to form the Harrowing of Hell.

But this myth is ill-founded. Matthew 27:52–53 is probably an

---

99. Harvey Cox, *The Secular City: Secularization and Urbanization in Theological Perspective* (New York: Macmillan, 1966).

embellished version of an earlier, simpler account of the results of the Good Friday earthquake that split boulders and broke open tombs, exposing the corpses interred there. Fearing this, their relatives came to check on the situation and, if need be, rebury them. But some redactor decided that wasn't sufficiently spectacular and rewrote it into a group resurrection, perhaps a clumsy attempt to display Christ's resurrection as the first fruits of the general, eschatological, resurrection.

First Peter 3:18–20 has been misread. "He was put to death in the body but made alive in the spirit *in which he* went to preach to the spirits who proved disobedient in the days of Noah." Keep in mind, the early manuscripts had no spacing between words, if you can believe it. The italicized phrase above, depending on how you divide the words *en ho kai*, could mean "in which he" *or* "Enoch." In the context, referring to Noah and the fallen Sons of God who provoked the Flood, it has to refer to the patriarch Enoch, who, in the course of his celestial journey, visited these Watchers, who pled with him to intercede for them with God. (No luck, though.) So it's not about Jesus at all.

Ephesians 4:8–10 is a fragment of Gnostic theology, whereby the Gnostic Redeemer, freed from his own captivity in the Netherworld, rescues the true spirits once stolen from him to vitalize the inert puppets of the Demiurge. This is almost a version of the Harrowing of Hell, but it presupposes a very different theological context than the one traditionally envisioned by Christians.

11

Faith and Works

Mutually Assured Destruction

There are always two foci to the topic of salvation, the *objective* (the saving event whereby Christ accomplished salvation for us), and the *subjective* (what we must do, if anything, to make that salvation our own). I have briefly dealt with the objective pole in my previous chapters. Here we will survey the major understandings of what we must do about it.

What would you say are the conditions of salvation, that is, if there *are* any conditions? According to Universalists, God has simply saved everyone, whether or not they have faith. If you did have faith you would be at an advantage in living a fuller life, and it would certainly give greater glory to Christ, but that's a different matter. For these reasons, it is still well worth taking the trouble to preach the gospel, even if no one's eternal salvation is going to be put at risk if you don't. There are different versions of the doctrine. A more traditional Universalism holds that Jesus died for everyone and—*it worked!* He didn't just *try* to save everyone. He died for the whole human race, so the whole human race is saved. (The same logic led second-generation Calvinists to suppose that Jesus must *not* have died for the whole human race, but only for the predestined elect.

This is the doctrine of the "Limited Atonement." But either way, he must have accomplished what he set out to do.)

According to "the second founder of Universalism," Hosea Ballou,[100] who was something of a Rationalist, God can have required no sacrifice and only sent Christ to die to reveal the absurdity of the whole notion. This is an idea with deep Pauline roots, having Christ die to expose and nullify the Torah (Col. 2:14–17).

Calvinists hold that God has sent Christ to die for the elect, whom he chose unconditionally. They are predestined to believe, and God himself supplies the act of faith by which they are saved (Eph. 2:8–9; Acts 13:48). Among the followers of Ramanuja in Visistadvaita Vedanta Hinduism, this is also the opinion of the Cat School, named for the tendency of mama cat to simply pick up her kittens by the scruff of the neck and carry them around. The same doctrine is found also in Jodo Shinsu Buddhism, where it is believed humans are so far gone in a degenerate age and so crushed beneath a load of bad karma that it takes the grace of Amida Buddha to be saved. Any inclination you feel to seek salvation is itself an exercise of Amida's saving grace toward you.

For Arminians (followers of Jacob Arminius, not members of the Armenian Orthodox Church), people are not so "totally depraved" (as Calvinists say) that they cannot recognize their need to be saved or reach out in faith to be saved. Whereas Calvinists would regard such self-generated faith leading to salvation as a saving work (and thus impossible), Arminians see it not as meritorious (in which case, they agree, it *would* be a saving work wrought in one's own strength), but rather the morally and salvifically neutral act of accepting a gift (as Billy Graham often said). Dietrich Bonhoeffer called repentance, even though it leads to salvation, a "dead work."[101] See Acts 2:40 and Mark 1:15. This idea of cooperating with God leads to *synergism*.

---

100. Ballou, *Treatise on Atonement*.

101. Dietrich Bonhoeffer, *The Cost of Discipleship*. Trans. R.H. Fuller (New York: Macmillan, 1963), p. 71.

Eastern Orthodox, Roman Catholics, and radical Arminians, though they would explain it in different ways, tend to believe that faith alone is not enough. Works, too, are required. Perhaps this is because all three groups view salvation as more of a process than a one-time event which settles things once and for all. See Romans 2:13; Philippians 2:12–13; and James 2:24. God's grace, to be sure, enables good works, but it remains your decision to cooperate, to yield to God's grace.

Roman Catholics view sacraments (especially baptism, penance, and the eucharist) as "means of grace," and that one needs such infusions on a regular basis, which is why excommunication, being cut off from the sacraments, would be a spiritual death sentence. Protestants are heading in the same direction, in practical terms, when they recognize that, if one neglects disciplines like regular prayer and Bible study, one is headed for spiritual atrophy.

Works of the Law

The range of opinions just summarized presuppose, most of them anyway, the terms in which Martin Luther defined the "faith versus works" issue. But in the last couple of decades the discussion has moved on, centering about the "new look" on the Apostle Paul anticipated by F.C. Baur[102] and really initiated by Krister Stendahl.[103] What if the issue treated in Romans and Galatians was not that of the relative weight of faith/belief and good moral deeds? What if the point was instead whether the ceremonial, ritual stipulations which

---

102. F.C. Baur, *Paul the Apostle of Jesus Christ: His Life and Works, His Epistles and Teachings: A Contribution to a Critical History of Early Christianity*. Trans. Eduard Zeller. Theological Translation Fund Library. (London: Williams & Norgate. Two Volumes, 1873–1875; rpt. Two Volumes in One, Peabody: Hendrickson Publishers, 2003).

103. Krister Stendahl, "The Apostle Paul and the Introspective Conscience of the West." In Stendahl, *Paul Among Jews and Gentiles and other Essays* (Philadelphia: Fortress Press, 1976), pp. 78–96. See also E.P. Sanders, *Paul, the Law, and the Jewish People* (Minneapolis: Fortress Press, 1983).

functioned to insulate Jews from the compromises of assimilation, were moot in the case of Gentile converts to Christianity? Would not the very phrase "works of *the Law*," i.e., the Torah, suggest this? No one thinks Paul believed commandments like "Thou shalt not kill" and "Thou shalt not commit adultery" were abrogated. (The writer of the Epistle of James seems to have thought so, but he, too, seems to invidiously misinterpret the "faith/works" dichotomy for polemics' sake.) And what about the Pauline references to an impending judgment facing believers for deeds done in the flesh (2 Cor. 5:10)? It is John, not Paul, who says, "He who believes in me will not face the judgment but has already passed from death into life." The Gospel of John (before the Ecclesiastical Redactor[104] got ahold of it!) teaches a completely realized eschatology (to be discussed in our final chapter), but Paul stops decidedly short of it.[105] You're not out of the woods yet!

These developments would seem to undermine the whole Protestant doctrine of salvation and the role of good works within it. Of course, that's only if anyone besides professional New Testament scholars took it seriously which, unfortunately, I doubt.

James versus Paul

The classic locus for harmonizing "apparent contradictions" is the seeming disagreement between the Epistle of James on the one hand and Romans and Galatians on the other. I refer to the texts and their authors by the traditional names even though the authorship question is not settled. We don't know for certain who actually wrote any of them. But the texts do seem opposed. Martin Luther certainly thought so. He streamlined the New Testament canon when he pre-

---

104. Rudolf Bultmann, *The Gospel of John:* pp. 219–220.

105. Ernst Käsemann, *Perspectives on Paul*. Trans. Margaret Kohl (Philadelphia: Fortress Press, 1971), chapter I, "On Paul's Anthropology," esp. pp. 2–4.

pared his German edition. The Epistle of James was one of the casualties. Why? Because Luther could see it failed to teach, and even taught against, the Pauline gospel of justification by grace through faith. Oh, sure, read it if you want. There's good stuff in there. But it fails the test for canonicity.

The author of James clearly has Romans open on the desk before him. James 2:14–26 is a point-for-point rejoinder to Romans 3:27–4:6.

Paul: Then what becomes of our boasting? It is excluded. On what principle? On the principle of works? No, but on the principle of faith. For we hold that a man is justified by faith apart from works of law. (Rom. 3:27–28)

James: What does it profit, my brethren, if a man says he has faith but has not works? Can his faith save him? [. . .] So faith by itself, if it has no works, is dead. (2:14, 17)

Paul: Or is God the God of Jews only? Is he not the God of Gentiles also? Yes, of Gentiles also, since God is one. (Rom. 3:29–30a)

James: You believe that God is one; you do well. Even the demons believe—and shudder. (Jas. 2:19)

Paul: What then shall we say about Abraham, our forefather according to the flesh? For if Abraham was justified by works, he has something to boast about, but not before God. For what does the scripture say? "Abraham believed God, and it was reckoned to him as righteousness." (Rom. 4:1–3)

James: Do you want to be shown, you shallow man, that faith apart from works is barren? Was not Abraham our father justified by works, when he offered his son Isaac upon the altar? You see that faith was active along with his works, and faith was completed by works, and the scripture was fulfilled which says, "Abraham believed God, and it was reckoned to him as righteousness." (2:20–23)

It looks as if James is firing over Paul's head, his opponent *in absentia*. He is contesting with a man long dead, just as Origen "debated" with Celsus, a Middle Platonist from a century and a half earlier. That might strike you as unfair, but then what are you as an author to do? If you feel compelled to respond to a text left by a previous author, why not? You just have to do your best not to misrepresent him. But James has, alas, misunderstood Paul. James has lost sight of the real issue in Romans and Galatians. Their author was talking about "works of *the law*," works required by the Torah, the ritual and dietary regulations whose purpose was to safeguard Jewish ethnicity over against Gentile assimilation. But James seems to think Paul means moral good deeds.

The only way out of this I can see is if James did understand the "ritual versus moral" distinction but thought that if you were willing to drop the ritual laws, nothing would stand in the way of you dropping the moral commandments, too. "For whosoever shall keep the whole law, and yet offend in one point, he is guilty of all. For he that said, 'Do not commit adultery,' said also, 'Do not kill.' Now if you do not commit adultery, but you do kill, you have [still] become a transgressor of the law." But I have to admit, I don't think this solves the problem, since both commandments James cites are moral in nature, neither being ritual.

If you think Martin Luther was going too far when he kicked James out of the New Testament, let me suggest that you are in effect doing the same thing when you pretend that James is, despite appearances, actually saying the same thing as Paul. At least Luther was honest about it.

Salvation by Cognitive Works

Tillich[106] and Bultmann[107] have stressed the need to extend the Protestant rejection of justification by works to include works of the *intellect*, the supposed virtue of believing unproveable assertions about miracles, doctrines, etc.

> Thus the basic principle of Protestantism, the principle of justification through faith, is applied to the question of truth. (Tillich)

> The step I myself made in these years was the insight that the principle of justification through faith refers not only to the religious-ethical but also to the religious-intellectual life. Not only he who is in sin but also he who is in doubt is justified through faith. (Tillich)

> [D]e-mythologizing is the radical application of the doctrine of justification by faith to the sphere of knowledge and thought. Like the doctrine of justification, de-mythologizing destroys any longing for security. There is no difference between security based on good works and security built on objectifying knowledge. (Bultmann)

Tillich says that the Christian must be seen not only as "justified though a sinner" but also "justified though a doubter." This is so, says Tillich, because faith is best understood as "ultimate concern," which means engagement with some question or cause, not the fragile superficiality of mere belief. The theologian is the one who wrestles with religious questions, not a spin doctor or cheer leader for a dogmatic party line. Not one who decides to believe, or forces himself to believe, that something happened (the resurrection) or didn't hap-

---

106. Paul Tillich, *The Interpretation of History*. Trans. N.A. Rasetzki and Elsa L. Talmey (New York: Scribners, 1936), p. 172; Tillich, *The Protestant Era*. Trans. James Luther Adams (Chicago: University of Chicago Press, 1948), p. xiv.

107. Bultmann, *Jesus Christ and Mythology*, p. 17.

pen (evolution). The person who esteems himself as one of the elect, one of the "saved," because he believes the right things is boasting of his achievements. He is (unwittingly) counting on salvation by cognitive works.

To put this a different way, picture yourself accepting Christ as your personal savior and joining a Christian congregation. But after some study and pondering, you confess that the Trinity makes no sense to you, or that you just cannot believe in the inerrancy of scripture. What do you think would happen? Your fellow members would call your questions "doubts" and would try their best to assuage them. If you remained unconvinced, you would be (tearfully) shown the door, having proven that you are no genuine Christian after all. But wait! Weren't you told that salvation comes by faith, not works? Then why are you getting kicked out for not buying certain doctrinal points? It was a case of bait and switch. Not consciously, of course, but most Christians have implicitly confused saving faith with accepting a whole creedal checklist. And why do your fellow congregants "happen" to agree on the beliefs their particular church espouses? "Why do you believe in the Trinity, Frank?" The true answer would have to be, "Because the people in this church are so nice."

So, to paraphrase Martin Luther, "Doubt boldly!"

12

Jesus Christ Supper Star

Holy Communion

Isn't it ironic that the Eucharist is supposed to be the great sacrament of Christian unity, and yet the wide variety of theories it has spawned have become so many *barriers* to Christian unity? "Oh, you don't explain communion the way I do? Then I'm sorry: I'm going to have to take my wafers and go home." If it's theoretically possible to divide over something, you can bet some Christians, somewhere, will split over it. One of the silliest examples I can think of occurred in the church I pastored (though not during my pastorate there). The congregation was what you'd expect in the affluent North Jersey town of Montclair, New Jersey: "progressive." At issue was the burning question of whether one ought to use Dietarily Incorrect white bread cubes for communion, or a mix of white and wheat. Thus the symbol of Christian unity was turned into a checkered symbol of *dis*unity!

Righteous Recipe

Many ingredients have gone into the Eucharistic tradition. I want to give the main ones a cursory examination in this chapter. We are always told the basic premise of the Lord's Supper was that of a continuation of the Passover meal. The Passover is generally remembered in the New Testament as the occasion for the last supper of Jesus, when the Lord's Supper was instituted (Mark 14:16; Matt. 26:18; Luke 22:15). But this seems premature. In fact earlier roots/sources are visible if you look closely enough. For one thing, Mark and Matthew make the Last Supper a Passover seder only by way of placing the scene (arbitrarily) into a larger narrative context of Jesus arranging for a Passover celebration. No one in the Supper scene makes the slightest mention of the events or customs of Passover. Luke must have noticed this in Mark and so inserts what the other two Synoptics pointedly lack: "I have earnestly desired to eat this Passover with you before I suffer" (Luke 22:15). John chapters 13–16 depict the Last Supper, but it is not said, even in the narrative context, to have been a Passover seder. In fact, John has Jesus die, not dine, on the day of Passover, at the very hour the Passover lambs were slaughtered. Actually, as Etienne Nodet and Justin Taylor show, even the canonical version itself points instead towards Pentecost, celebrated at Qumran with bread and wine every fifty days. Remember, Pentecost commemorated the giving of the Torah to Moses on Mount Sinai.

> Allusions to the Covenant and to blood (Matt 26:29 par.) strike a note which does not appear to be directly related to Passover, since there is no connection with the lamb, not even with the blood rite of Exod12:22 f. On the other hand, it has been noted for a long time now that the "Covenant blood" of Matt and Mark alludes to the sacrifice that seals the revelation at Sinai (Exod 24:8.)[108]

---

108. Etienne Nodet and Justin Taylor, *The Origins of Christianity: An Exploration*. A Michael Glazier Book (Collegeville: Liturgical Press, 1998), pp. 112–113.

Alfred Loisy[109] discerned in the Words of Institution a liturgical coloring in the utterance "This is my body. . . . This is my blood."

> We can see at once that the words "This is my body" would be utterly unintelligible for a reader unacquainted with the Christian Eucharist. Clearly then he is supposed to be acquainted with it. . . . All this would be intelligible enough to a Christian reader familiar with the developed eucharistic rite as practiced in the group for which the Gospel was intended: but perfectly unintelligible on the occasion when the sayings are supposed to have been uttered. . . . These mystic sayings have no natural sense except for referring to an accepted Christian sacrament, and as explaining it.

Here we are reading a ritual script as the celebrant explains to the congregation the symbolic significance, piece by piece, of the ceremonial elements. It just does not sound like conversational speech, either casual or grave. To see this, one need only compare the gospel version with some of the cinematic portrayals of the gospel scene. While some are in effect just filmings of people reciting the stilted lines from the gospel text, others try to paraphrase it into plausible conversation, even embroidering it with extended context, but even then it sounds artificial, unnatural.

> This is my blood you drink, this is my body you eat; if you would remember me when you eat and drink. . . . I must be mad thinking I'll be remembered! I must be out of my *head!* Look at your blank faces! My name will mean nothing ten minutes after I'm dead![110]

> Now drink this wine. Pass the cup. This wine is my blood. Do this to remember me.[111]

---

109. Alfred Loisy, *The Birth of the Christian Religion*. Trans. L.P. Jacks (London: George Allen & Unwin, 1948), p. 249.

110. Tim Rice, *Jesus Christ Superstar*.

111. Paul Schraeder and Martin Scorcese, *The Last Temptation of Christ*.

Albert Schweitzer[112] realized that the gospel accounts of the Last Supper were products of literary-liturgical artistry, but he believed there *was* a historical core to it. He (Jesus *or* Schweitzer, take your pick) saw it in eschatological terms. The original element had nothing to do with redemptive sacrifice. Rather, it boiled down to the so-called Vow of Abstinence: "Truly, I say to you, I shall not drink again of the fruit of the vine until that day when I drink it new in the kingdom of God" (Mark 14:25). Schweitzer thought Jesus did not mean he was swearing off the booze for the unknown duration till the eschaton, as a kind of hunger strike. No, the intent was to say that you could measure the (very short) time till the End of the Age by counting down to Happy Hour! It would be a parallel to another saying just a chapter earlier: "From the fig tree learn its lesson: as soon as its branch becomes tender and puts forth its leaves, you know that summer is near. So also, when you see these things taking place, you know that he is near, at the very gates" (Mark 13:28–29). Joachim Jeremias[113] saw this, too:

> By a solemn vow of abstinence He forswears all feasts and wine for the future, so as to set before His disciples and impart to them His own complete certainty that the final consummation is near at hand.

Ditto Bultmann:[114]

---

112. Albert Schweitzer, *The Problem of the Lord's Supper according to the Scholarly Research of the Nineteenth Century and the Historical Accounts.* Trans. Andrew J. Mattill, Jr. (Macon: Mercer University Press, 1982), pp. 136–137; Schweitzer, *The Kingdom of God and Primitive Christianity.* Trans. L.A. Garrard (New York: Seabury Press, 1968), p. 146.

113. Joachim Jeremias, *The Eucharistic Words of Jesus.* Trans. Arnold Ehrhardt (Oxford: Basil Blackwell, 1955), p. 172.

114. Rudolf Bultmann, *The History of the Synoptic Tradition.* Trans. John Marsh (New York: Harper & Row, rev. ed., 1963), p. 266.

It had originally been told how Jesus at a (ceremonial? The last?) meal expressed the certainty of his eating the next (festival) meal in the Kingdom of God, and then expected it to happen in the immediate future.

But I have an alternative suggestion. I envision the saying as originating in the early Christian encratite movements (Marcionites, Gnostics, etc.) who preached the celibacy gospel. They believed that the primordial transgression of Adam and Eve was sexual intercourse, and that salvation meant, in the words of a psalmist, "We've got to get ourselves back to the Garden," swearing off sex even within marriage. Encratism (from Greek *enkrateo*, "self-control, continence") is on display in the Apocryphal Acts of John, Paul, and Thomas. "Blessed are the continent, for to them shall God speak" (Acts of Paul, chapter 5). Encratites were also egalitarians, pacifists, vegetarians, anarchists, *teetotalers*, and *apocalyptists* looking for a soon-coming Parousia. The Mark 14:25 logion makes the most sense to me as an initiatory pledge to shun the wineskin until the Messianic Banquet, probably not far off. It would be comparable to a similarly tendentious saying ascribed to Jesus by the Ebionites: "I came to abolish sacrifices, and if you do not cease from sacrificing, the wrath of my Father shall not cease from you."

It seems pretty clear that originally the Eucharistic liturgy had nothing to do with Jesus' death. If it had, how can we explain the existence of the version preserved in the *Didache* ("The Teaching of the Twelve Apostles," a late first-century or early second-century Syrian church manual)?

But as touching the eucharistic thanksgiving, give thanks thus. First, as regards the cup: We give You thanks, O our Father, for the holy vine of Your son David, which You made known to us through Your Son Jesus; Yours is the glory for ever and ever. Then as regards the broken bread: We give You thanks, O our Father, for the life and knowledge which You made known to us through Your Son Jesus; Yours is the glory for ever and ever. As this broken bread was scattered on the mountains and being gathered together became one, so may Your Church be gathered together from the ends of the earth into Your kingdom. (*Didache* 9:1–8, J.B. Lightfoot trans.)

This sounds purely Jewish-Christian, altogether innocent of any atonement theology. So where did the redemptive death business come from? The answer, though theologically abhorrent to many, is by no means far to seek. It simply must have been the influence of the Hellenistic Mystery Religions, most of which offered a sacramental initiation whereby one reenacted the mythic victory of the cult's dying and rising deity. Such religions included the cults of Mithras, Isis and Osiris, and Dionysus. The Christian sacrament most closely resembled those of Osiris and Dionysus, two fertility gods whose devotees ritually partook of their bodies and blood. You see, as fertility gods each one's body was bread, the "body" of the grain," and his blood was the "blood" of the grape (wine) or of the grain (beer). ("Thou art wine, yet thou art not wine, but the members of Osiris."[115] "May this wine become the blood of Osiris."[116]) These features of the Christian communion meal demonstrate that whoever added them understood Jesus, the True Vine, to be a "corn king" like his pagan rivals. You tell me what any of this has to do with the Jewish Passover. Clearly, that connection is a case of (secondary) Judaizing.

Why is such thinking so distasteful to conventional Christian historians? It must be because they want Christianity to have fallen out of heaven with no human fingerprints on it. "Flesh and blood has

---

115. From a magical papyrus in the British Museum, quoted in Francis Legge, *Forerunners and Rivals of Christianity from 330 B.C. to 330 A.D.* (New Hyde Park, NY: University Books, 1964), p. 87.

116. From an Egyptian love charm quoted in Legge, *Forerunners and Rivals.*

not revealed it to you, but my Father who is in heaven" (Matt. 16:17). "I would have you know, brothers, that the gospel that was preached by me is not man's gospel. For I did not receive it from any man, nor was I taught it, but I received it through a revelation of Jesus Christ" (Gal. 1:11–12). If Christianity is man-made, it is merely "good views, not good news" from Beyond. Paul Tillich[117] explains that

> the concept of religion dissolves the unconditionality of revelation into the continuous evolution and alteration within the history of religion and culture. "Religion" as a general concept is indifferent to the revelatory claims of the particular religions.

This is why you find statements like these from adherents of all the religions.[118]

> The attempt to reduce Judaism to a religion is a betrayal of its true nature. (Milton Steinberg)

> We must reject the assumption that Judaism is, or can be reduced to, a religion only. (Mordecai M. Kaplan)

> It is hardly possible . . . to determine whether [Hinduism] is a religion or not. (Jawaharlal Nehru)

> Hinduism is not a codified religion but a geographical term. Pluralism is the root nature of Hinduism. You may belong to any religion and still be a Hindu. (Akshat Gupta)

> Buddhism is not a religion in the sense in which that word is commonly understood. (Maha Thera U Thittula)

---

117. Paul Tillich, "The Conquest of the Concept of Religion in the Philosophy of Religion." In Tillich, *What Is Religion?* Trans. and ed., James Luther Adams. Harper Torchbooks (New York: Harper & Row, 1973), p. 127.

118. Quotes 1, 2, 3, 5, and 7 are assembled in Wilfred Cantwell Smith, *The Meaning and End of Religion: A New Approach to the Religious Traditions of Mankind.* A Mentor Book (New American Library, 1964), p. 115.

Buddhism is a philosophy of life, not a religion. (Rajat Parjapat)

Islam is not merely a "religion" in the sense in which this term is understood in the West. (Said Ramadan)

Islam is not a religion. Islam is a movement of justice. (Saif Mohammad)

Christianity is not a religion; it's a relationship. (ubiquitous bumper sticker)

Christianity is not a religion but a way of life, a falling in love with God, and through him a falling in love with our fellows. (John Bertram Phillips)

I see in all this an absolutely perfect example of Jacques Derrida's *iteration paradox*.[119] Derrida observes that a unique thing, idea, whatever, can be understood only once it has been repeated, multiplied, reiterated. Only then is it possible for us to categorize it, to understand the *kind* of thing it is. "Ah! One of *those!*" In just this way, we can only begin to understand what our religion is—at the price of admitting ours is just one of many.

Feed Me Till I Want No More

We read of various early Christian groups who celebrated the Lord's

---

119. Once it contains the possibility of iteration (having an imitable "shape") a thing both gains and loses its essence since it invites its own vicarious displacement. *Representation presupposes deferral, its no-longer-presence.* See the discussion in Rodolphe Gasche, *The Tain of the Mirror: Derrida and the Philosophy of Reflection* (Cambridge: Harvard University Press, 1986), pp. 212–217; Jacques Derrida, "The Double Session." In Derrida, *Dissemination.* Trans. Barbara Johnson (Chicago: University of Chicago Press, 1981), pp. 234–235; Derrida, "Signature Event Context." In Derrida, *Margins of Philosophy.* Trans. Alan Bass (Chicago: University of Chicago Press, 1982), pp. 323–324; Derrida, "Limited Inc. a b c . . ." Trans. Samuel Weber. In Derrida, *Limited Inc* (Evanston: Northwestern University Press, 1988), pp. 61–62.

Supper with water instead of wine, with fish instead of any drink, etc., a phenomenon implying that the familiar routine of sharing in bread and wine was not a given from the start, but rather a later standardization from the top down. The situation is in some ways parallel to that of the New Testament canon, with a competition between local versions to produce a unifying standard. Not that either has ever been completely successful: even today some of the ancient Apostolic Orthodox Churches (Ethiopian, Coptic, Armenian, etc.) still have somewhat different canons of scripture, and a few denominations including the Kimbanguist Church of Congo (Kinshasa), the Society of Friends , or Quakers, and the Salvation Army, have no sacraments at all. The vast majority of Christian denominations do practice communion and baptism, and the variety of theological explanations is amazing.

Roman Catholics, of course, espouse the famous doctrine of *Transubstantiation.* There is good reason to think that the "real presence" of Christ, however defined, had long been dominant in historical Christianity. The second-century author of the Ignatian epistles characterized the eucharist as "the medicine of immortality." First Corinthians 10:1–4 refers to the communion bread and wine as akin to the manna and the water sprung from solid rock, both constituting "spiritual food" and "spiritual drink" capable of *killing* any who approached the sacrament in an inappropriate spirit (1 Cor. 11:27–30).

John's gospel documents a running battle between scribes belonging to two opposed factions. Sometimes ancient scribes just omitted material they didn't like or deemed heretical, but other times they did not feel at liberty to remove text. In that case, they would add "corrective" material to promote their own opinions, figuring that readers would read the new stuff and think, "Oh! I thought John was saying so-and-so, but now I see I must have misunderstood!"[120]

---

120. This isn't just a lot of Higher-Critical speculation; it's precisely what John the Revelator had in mind: "I warn every one who hears the words of the

Thus we have the original Gnosticizing version in which Jesus, in a Marcionitish (cf. 6:46) mood, denigrates the Old Testament story of Moses and the manna in favor of his own, far superior, "bread," his saving revelation (John 6:31–33, 47–51a; cf. Prov. 9:1–6). But this was not good enough for the catholicizing Ecclesiastical Redactor, who has added, in verses 51b-56, a heavily sacramental rejoinder in which the material elements of the Eucharist are made the secret of Christian salvation, Ignatius' "medicine of immortality." One must "eat," or, literally translated, "chew, masticate" the very flesh of the Son of Man. "For my flesh is real food, my blood real drink." But the ball springs back over the net, as a rival scribe adds: "It is the spirit that gives life; the flesh counts for nothing. The words that I have spoken to you are spirit and life" (6:63). *Get that, folks? The spirit, not the flesh!* Here we have a vivid anticipation of the dispute between Luther and Zwingli, to be discussed below.

It was the great philosopher-saint Thomas Aquinas[121] who defined Transubstantiation by the use of Aristotelian categories. The problem he tackled was how the body of Christ could sit enthroned beside his Father up in heaven and yet also rest upon every church altar throughout Christendom every Sunday. This is how he did it. Aristotle had theorized a distinction between the *essence* and the *accidents* of a thing. The essence is the defining nature of a thing, while the accidents are the qualities, the properties, the characteristics of the thing. The essence is interior and invisible, while the accidents

---

prophecy of this book: if any one adds to them, God will add to him the plagues described in this book, and if any one takes away from the words of the book of this prophecy, God will take away his share in the tree of life and in the holy city, which are described in this book." Similarly, in 1 Enoch, the patriarch blesses those who will "write out all my words exactly in their languages, and do not alter or omit anything from my words, but write out everything exactly" (CIV:11), M.A. Knibb trans. They knew it was likely to happen! In case you hadn't noticed, this is exactly what Matthew and Luke did to Mark's "Little Apocalypse" (Mark 13).

121. Whenever I am tempted to think how much smarter I am than all these "unenlightened" believers, my mind flashes back to intellectual titans like Aquinas and Barth, and I realize what a dullard I really am!

are external, visible. The essence and the accidents always agree. The externals tell you what the essence is. "If it looks like a duck, walks like a duck, and quacks like a duck, then it probably *is* a duck."

But there is one single instance in which the essence does *not* match the accidents: the Eucharistic bread and wine as consecrated by the priest during the mass. Once that happens, the bread and wine lose their essence *as* bread and wine and instead take on the essence of the body and blood of the Risen Jesus. But the accidents (e.g., the chemical composition, volume, taste) remain those of bread and wine. This is why only stupid wise-ass jerks carp that Catholics believe that in taking communion they are chomping on Jesus' fingernails or his pancreas. Of course that is not what the Catholic Church teaches.

However, I see a problem with what they *do* teach. Did Aquinas really explain anything? "Oh, Transubstantation happens by a *miracle*, you say! *Now* I get it!" Oh no, you *don't*. This is just like the wonderful cartoon by S. Harris in which a scientist is explaining his blackboard-filling theorem to a colleague who remains a tad skeptical. The latter points to an empty circle chalked in the middle of all the figures. An arrow connects the circle with the words "Then a miracle occurs." He says, "I think you should be more explicit here in step two." Isn't that what Aquinas was saying? You want to "explain" one conundrum by another one? Be my guest.

Lutherans and some Anglicans believe in what is called *sacramental union*. The notion of "real presence" has moved from the interior of the bread and wine to their grace-imparting function.

> But the act of Communion not only brings the faithful all the benefits which Our Lord has won for them on Calvary, it is a true fruition of the Body of Christ, making the soul really and truly one with its Lord. The union is a foretaste, a preparation for the beatific vision. (G.W.O. Addleshaw)[122]

---

122. G.W.O. Addleshaw, *The High Church Tradition: A Study in the Liturgical Thought of the Seventeenth Century* (London: Faber and Faber, 1941),

The Anglican Lollards (late fourteenth century) pioneered the near-Catholic doctrine of *Consubstantiation* (frequently and erroneously ascribed to Lutherans). "Trans-" denotes a change from one condition to another; "con-" denotes "with." Accordingly, Consubstantiation is much like its Catholic counterpart except that the belief is that the bread and wine do not lose their original essence, but instead take on a second essence: that of the body and blood of Christ. So it's both at the same time, sort of like Jesus himself: one person with two natures.

Some Anglicans/Episcopalians hold to a purposely vague notion of the "real presence" of Christ in the communion elements. I think of the claim of Muslim theologians of the Hanbalite school that Allah possesses humanoid bodily members but "without how."[123]

Calvinists are at least *supposed* to believe that the Holy Spirit is present in the communion service, causing the spirits of communicants to ascend invisibly to Christ enthroned in heaven where their nature is united with the human (not divine, mind you) nature of Christ. This one strikes me as somehow even more contrived than Aristotelian Transubstantiation. Granted, it took some ingenuity to cook this up, but is there any real reason to believe this was happening of a Sunday at your local Presbyterian or Dutch Reformed Church? If it was actually *experienced* as a visionary journey, that would be something else again, but that's not what they say is happening. And can you picture something like this in your local Ludlow Bushmat Memorial Presbyterian Church? Not me.[124]

---

pp, 105–106.

123. Ignaz Goldziher, *An Introduction to Islamic Theology and Law*. Trans. Andras and Ruth Hamori. Modern Classics in Near Eastern Studies (Princeton: Princeton University Press, 1981), p. 92.

124. Once I was attending a friend's Presbyterian Church in Athens, Georgia. Not surprisingly, it was no great shakes. I was idly looking over the church bulletin they passed out to help you keep up with the program. At the end, it piously declared "We go forth to serve," to which I pen-added the word "lunch."

Martin Luther and Huldreich Zwingli, leaders, respectively, of the German and Swiss Reformation movements, once met for merger negotiations, but there turned out to be a sticking point the two Reformers just couldn't get past. Predictably, it was their inability to agree on the meaning of the Eucharist. It came down to that sage remark by President Bill Clintion: "It depends on what the meaning of 'is' is." What precisely did it mean when Jesus said, "This *is* my body; this *is* my blood"? Luther insisted that "'is' means 'is'!" Thus some version of Real Presence. But Zwingi replied, in effect, "Dontcha know a metaphor when ya *see* one?" That was the end of that. They agreed on salvation by grace through faith, but that wasn't good enough. Oh well . . .

This all may be moot today, when, as I strongly suspect, both Catholic and Protestant laity lack the faintest idea what beliefs their denominational labels stand for. Personally, I'm torn. As a fan of Historical Theology, I hate to see these venerable creeds die away, On the other hand, as an advocate of Free Thought, the last thing I want to see is *indoctrination*. But I would love to see *education* in one's inherited religious tradition, combined with the encouragement to make one's own studied decision whether to stick with it or not. To me, that's the best of both worlds.

13

Scriptural Authority versus the Bible
I said it! God believes it! That settles it!

If God reveals things to us, how does he do it? Traditionally, theologians have spoken of *"general revelation."* This is the idea that God is manifest to us in the design and the grandeur of the world *and* in religious experience (in any religion). There are several Christian opinions as to how effective or valuable general revelation is, compared to *special revelation* (miracles, heavenly voices, scriptural inspiration, etc.).

The *Gnostic* view is that there *is* no general revelation since God did not create the world in the first place! We must have special revelation to know about the true God at all. True Gnostics possess the divine spark within, but even this does not enable them to know about God or to experience him in the soul—until special revelation from the Gnostic Revealer supervenes to awaken the spark. Until then, the divinity within only makes us feel uneasy in this alien world, telling us something is amiss. Thus the divine spark plays a role analogous to the Law in Lutheran theology. And it is the same in Samkhya Hinduism, where life in this world is awful precisely in order to push us to look for something better.

The *Reformed* view, that, e.g., of John Calvin and Karl Barth, is that there *is* a general revelation, but original sin has blinded our eyes to it. We cannot really see it for what it is until the special revelation of Jesus Christ's gospel provides "spectacles" for us to put on and see.

The *Thomist* view (that of Thomas Aquinas) is that there is a general revelation available to all people, even sinners and pagans, but it is not adequate for salvation. Aristotle rightly deduced the existence of a Creator God and the requirements of a moral life, but reason alone, based on general revelation, cannot provide the necessary knowledge that God is a Trinity, has a Son, or has provided a plan of salvation. We need special revelation for that.

The Liberal view of theologians Schubert Ogden,[125] Fritz Buri,[126] David Tracy, [127]and others is that general revelation is available to all *and* is adequate to salvation. What special revelation does is to *re-present* general revelation in a conspicuous form. Some would say that special revelation merely explains how God saves, even though one may be saved without knowing how it works. (Abraham's faith, or that of a South Sea Islander, saves him, but they needn't (because they *can't*) know God has revealed that it is the death of Christ that makes such faith operative.)

The view of Deists and advocates of "natural religion" such as Thomas Paine and Ethan Allen was that there is *only* general revelation, *no* special revelation! God has revealed himself in nature, not scripture, and he has given us reason as the only necessary "spectacles." Hence the title of Ethan Allen's great book *Reason the Only Oracle of Man.*

---

125. Schubert M. Ogden, *The Reality of God and Other Essays* (New York: Harper & Row, 1966).

126. Fritz Buri, *Christian Faith in Our Time.* Trans. Edward Allen Kent (New York: Macmillan), 1966; Buri, *Theology of Existence.* Trans. Harold H. Oliver and Gerhard Onder (Greenwood, SC: Attic Press, 1965).

127. David Tracy, *Blessed Rage for Order: The New Pluralism in Theology* (New York: Seabury Press, 1978).

Special Revelation

I like the way Karl Barth described special revelation, as the intrusion of a bolt of objective truth into the clashing echoes of subjective human belief and opinion. A ray of light penetrating the foggy shadows of delusion. Biblically, there are several methods of such communication. One of the major ones is *prophecy*.[128] Inspired spokesmen are given messages for some human audience, whether they want to hear the message or not! A similar phenomenon is the consulting of *oracles*. Messages are obtained for inquirers through verbal or nonverbal methods. The latter include the dice-like Urim and Thummim and the Ephod, some sort of a breastplate or image. *Miracles*, also called "signs" may symbolize revealed truths or verify them, as when Jesus points to his healing the lame man to prove his/our authority to forgive sins.

Incarnation is of course a prime means of revelation, since you're getting divine truth right from the horse's mouth. God becomes a man (or theoretically a woman, as with Mother Ann Lee). Would the teachings of such an avatar automatically be infallible? Hard to say! Kenotic theology says the divine being's knowledge would, like his powers, be set aside for the duration of the incarnation. He wouldn't necessarily know much better than we do! A variant version would be a *theophany*, a docetic ("apparent") incarnation, in which God appears in a human form, albeit an insubstantial one. The same as an angelophany, but it is God appearing in human form.

Scriptural inspiration is just as important in its own way, since we do not have the opportunity anymore to question God directly, but we do have the Bible. Inspiration is divine guidance, uplifting, or enlightenment of the editorial judgment of a scriptural writer. *Also* the subtle and unnoticed supply of knowledge, or guidance of speculation or reasoning, of a biblical author. Inspiration means, literally,

---

128. May I point out that the noun form is "prophecy," with a "c." The verb form is "to prophesy," with an "s." And to "prophesize" is slang.

"God-breathed," i.e., produced directly by divine initiative. This is a striking image, the implications of which, however, are not obvious.

Both the Old and New Testaments have various activities and powers inspired by God including *artistic skill* (Exod. 35:30–35), *military prowess and superhuman strength* (Judg. 3:10; 11:29; 14:6, 19; 15:14); *music* (1 Chron. 25:1–5; 1 Cor. 14:26; Col. 3:16), *glossolalia* (Acts 2:4; 1 Cor. 12:10; 2 Sam. 10:10–13); and, of course, *prophecy.* The inspiration of prophets as *inspired speakers* became attached imperceptibly and slowly to the written books containing their oracles. The inspiration of their contents gradually seeped into their form, the written texts. This "scriptural" inspiration was gradually expanded to cover all biblical books. But it seems to me sloppy and even misleading to take "Word of God" texts referring to *spoken* prophecies or the *preached* gospel and to quote them as if they were referring to written texts. Fundamentalists do this all the time when they talk about "the Bible's doctrine of itself" and quote references to "the Word of God" as if they referred to a book. Thus if we are to get a proper idea of a biblical doctrine of scripture, we have to look for statements by *later writers* reflecting back upon *earlier writings*, not just on prophecies or promises in general.

Philo and the Epistle of Aristeas tell the legend of the translation of the Hebrew Bible into Greek (the Septuagint). They say that scripture was translated simultaneously by 35 two-man teams of scholars, and that when they finally came together to compare results, the translations were identical! Hence the translation was as inspired as the original Hebrew. Similarly, in 4 Ezra 14:21–22, 38–48, we read that all Jewish scripture had been destroyed during the Babylonian Exile. God told Ezra to drink a revelatory potion, after which he entered the inspired state and dictated the whole scripture, word for word the same as it was, as well as another 72 esoteric scriptures!

Allegorical, Pesher, and Midrashic methods of esoteric interpretation of scripture imply a deeper layer that God's inspiration of every word made possible and worth seeking (see Gal. 3:16; Matt.

13:26–27; 13:51–52). Similarly, *the interpenetration of the categories "law" and "prophecy"* shows that *all* scripture is thought of as being inspired like an oracle (Rom. 3:2) and binding like a law (see John 10:34–5 quoting Psalm 82:6 as "unbreakable"). It is not uncommon in the New Testament to find "scripture says" and "God says" used interchangeably (Matt.19:4; 1 Cor. 6:16; Acts 13:34; Heb. 1:5; Rom. 9:17), which of course means that God speaks the words of scripture at every point. Second Peter 1:20–21 identifies prophets with their books and says the writers (implicitly, given the context, which treats of "private interpretation," i.e., of *texts*) were "carried along by the Spirit of God." Likewise, 2 Timothy 3:15–17 says, "All scripture is God-breathed," etc.

The early and medieval Church embraced the *dictation* model of scriptural inspiration. Philo's view is repeated by Christians: biblical writers wrote in a trance state, automatic writing, like a passive flute being played by God. Augustine said that a biblical writer is "a secretary for God, who must provide him with a graceful style as well as with the content of his writings." Origen: "The sacred books are not the works of men, but . . . they were composed and have come down to us as a result of the inspiration of the Holy Spirit." Origen recognized three levels of meaning liable to be found in any verse of scripture, something possible only if the text came from God by verbal inspiration. He admitted that the surface, historical sense might be in error, a red light to alert the reader to go deeper and seek some more profound level.

Thomas Aquinas distinguished between prophecy (or revelation) and inspiration. The first imparts new knowledge and thus affects the *intellect*. The second affects the *judgment*, causing the writer to make good use of information he already has or gains from some worldly source, not directly revealed (e.g., historical records, contemporary reports, interviews).

The Protestant Reformation

Martin Luther distinguished a *canon within the canon*. Writings are authoritative only insofar as they "preach and bear Christ" by which he meant: if they teach the doctrine of justification by grace through faith. Luther admitted that some books (e.g., James, Jude, Hebrews, Revelation) did *not*, and he relegated them to an appendix to the New Testament. But this applies to the question of canon—which books belong in the Bible—not to inspiration, the quality of a book that makes it canonical. For books that did make it into the canon, Luther felt they must be infallible and inerrant. At the same time, however, he had eliminated Origen's safety valve; Luther rejected all appeal to hidden, secret, allegorical meanings to which Origen could point as the infallible sense if it did not bear out as accurate in its literal sense. Luther insisted on the "grammatico-historical method," reading the Bible as if it were any other ancient text, no special rules or methods.

John Calvin believed scripture had been "dictated" and thus he felt obliged to harmonize biblical contradictions where he found them. On the other hand, he believed in "accommodationism," that scripture spoke in pre-scientific terms so as not to confuse ancient readers who did not know any better. Similarly, scripture, for Calvin, spoke anthropomorphically, using human metaphors for God, referring to his "throne," his "arms," etc., when in fact God must be beyond all this.

Leonardus Lessius, a seventeenth-century Flemish Jesuit, set forth three proposals: 1) *content inspiration*: God provided the thoughts for the biblical writers but left the expression to them; 2) *concomitant* inspiration: a divine superintendence resulting in freedom from error, but the initiative is human; 3) *consequent* inspiration: a writing initiated by humans and carried out without divine aid, that happened nonetheless to be inerrant and could *subsequently* be accepted by God as scripture. This was pretty daring thinking (and in many quarters still is).

Revisions and even rejection of biblical inspiration followed in the aftermath of the Higher Criticism of the eighteenth and nineteenth centuries. Archeology, critical historical method, source analysis, etc., indicated that the Bible was a collection of pre-scientific, mythical, legendary, propagandistic writings. Most were of uncertain or pseudonymous authorship, heavily redacted and interpolated. In light of all this, what could "inspiration" possibly mean?

Fundamentalism was one reaction. Princeton theologians Archibald Alexander Hodge and Benjamin Breckenridge Warfield taught "verbal inspiration" and "divine-human confluence." God prepared the writers with their own individual brains, skills, and styles. He then prompted them to write the various biblical documents and controlled them in their writing, and yet the initiative was equally their own. Inspiration is thus a special case of *predestination.* (Ironically, many non-Calvinists, who do not otherwise believe predestination makes any sense, suddenly adopt it here!) So scripture is inerrant, since God could not err or allow error. Scripture is not dictated, but the result is exactly the same as if it had been. That's having your manna and eating it, too.

Some verbal inspirationists (Protestants and Catholics alike) have restricted inspiration or inerrancy to only the moral, spiritual, religious, and doctrinal statements of the text, allowing that on irrelevant "secular" matters scripture might indeed err.

Modernists (again, among both Protestants and Catholics), unlike Warfield and Hodge, took seriously the results of Higher Criticism. Modernists/Liberals said that the Bible is inspired in the sense that its writers were religious geniuses, at least most of them, most of the time. (It is the implied unevenness in quality of the Bible that led Fundamentalists in reaction to frame the doctrine of not only verbal but also "plenary" inspiration, i.e., the whole thing's equally inspired.)

Liberals also saw the great goal of the Bible as to preserve the spiritual experiences of the ancients, and to record the evolution ("progressive revelation") of it, so as to provide us a gallery of examples and possibilities for the experiences we, too, might have with God. So the Bible is simultaneously the self-revelation of God *to* humanity and the gradual discovery of more and more of God *by* humanity.[129] Jesus was upheld by Liberals as the great example of piety.[130] They spoke of the "religion *of* Jesus" (centered upon the Father) rather than the "religion *about* Jesus" (centered upon the Son), seeing the latter as a dogmatic corruption of the former.

Neo-Orthodoxy was more conservative than Liberal Modernism, and indeed a reaction to it, though not as severe as Fundamentalism. The Neo-Orthodox (Karl Barth, Emil Brunner, et al.) stressed that God is not simply "discovered" in human religious experience but that rather God addresses humanity through his *Word* spoken through the prophets and paramountly in Jesus Christ, the incarnate Word of God. This Word is present in the Bible but is not identical with the text of the Bible. One might say it is identical with the gospel message. So the Bible *contains* the Word of God and even *becomes* the Word of God as one reads it under the influence of the Spirit.[131] But it would be idolatrous to say that the Bible *is* the Word of God.[132]

To put it another way, some Neo-Orthodox theologians (e.g., Donald M. Baillie) said that God reveals *himself*, not information

129. Harry Emerson Fosdick, *The Modern Use of the Bible* (New York: Macmillan, 1961), p. 30: "The underside of the process is man's discovery; the upper side is God's revelation."

130. Harry Emerson Fosdick, *The Personality of Jesus—The Soul of Christianity*. A Sermon Preached at Temple Beth-El, New York, Sunday, April 13, 1930.

131. Colin Brown, *Karl Barth and the Christian Message*. A Tyndale Paperback (Chicago: Inter-Varsity Press, 1967), pp. 32 ff; Herbert Hartwell, *The Theology of Karl Barth: An Introduction* (Philadelphia: Westminster Press, 1964), pp. 62–63.

132. Paul Tillich, *Dynamics of Faith*. World Perspectives Series vol. X. Harper Torchbooks (New York: Harper & Row, 1958), p. 52: "Faith, if it takes its symbols literally, becomes idolatrous!"

about himself or anything else. Brunner wrote a book called *Truth as Encounter*, reflecting the heavy Existentialist influence upon Neo-Orthodoxy.

It is important to understand: no Fundamentalist or traditional Roman Catholic theologian would deny that the Bible presents examples for us to follow, that it catalyzes encounters with God, that it contains and communicates the Word of God. It is not that the belief in the verbal, plenary inspiration of the Bible is in any way incompatible with any of these things. The point of contrast between the various views of biblical inspiration and authority is that, if one takes seriously the findings of biblical criticism, the Bible is simply no longer credible as the supernatural answer book traditional theology made it. Is it still possible to believe in the plenary, verbal inspiration of scripture, and that it is inerrant and infallible, whether on religio-moral issues or mundane issues? Liberal Modernists, Neo-Orthodox, and others say it is not, and they are engaging in "damage control." What is left to say, realistically, about biblical inspiration and authority?

The Authority of Biblical Revelation

It seems that the earliest natural response to a body of scripture by a religious community is to revere it as having literally been divinely dictated. But, sooner or later, someone in the community begins to face up to the human characteristics of the sacred writing. Eventually, the historical-cultural conditioning of the scripture will become apparent to some. This is starting to occur among Muslim theologians, and it has created theological havoc in Christianity. The pendulum has swung to both extremes, some theologians maximizing the human element in the Bible, others practically ignoring it. I would like to consider the question, first, from an evangelical perspective. By this we mean that position that accepts the authority and inspiration of the Bible, based, evangelicals insist, on the objectively determined historicity of the biblical documents. Because they give us a reliable record of the deeds and revelations of God, particularly the incarnation, we should heed the scriptural revelation that the Bible itself is inspired and authoritative.

I want to explore the question of just how different divinely revealed truth must be from humanly-discovered truth. I also want to see what the "phenomena of scripture" (i.e., the things we actually encounter as we read, like it or not) have to tell us about the nature of biblical revelation and its relation to biblical inspiration.

Progressive Revelation and Biblical Theology

Evangelical and fundamentalist laypersons frequently seek to demonstrate the inspiration (and authority) of the Bible by pointing out that, though written over a period of two thousand years and by over forty different authors, the Bible speaks with one voice. Aside from the fact that this would be not altogether remarkable since all of the authors wrote in a common religious tradition, this argument is rather circular. It shows us a very important theological and hermeneutical problem. It is assumed that God would never contradict himself in any revelation he gave (beside the fact that we would never know what to believe if he *did* contradict himself). It must be admitted that this is a natural and reasonable position to hold, but does it take adequate cognizance of all the factors involved in biblical revelation? Truly, "God is not man," including every one of those forty inspired authors. Could *they* contradict themselves (or each other) in writing down the God-given revelation, that is, if inspiration is other than verbal inspiration or dictation? This, of course, is the question of the role played by human authors as the mediators of God's revelation. If an examination of the Bible seems to indicate that such contradictions do exist, one would have to ask how this phenomenon is theologically to be dealt with in order to square it with that already established "given" of inspiration and authority. I love the way Clark

Pinnock once put it: "Fundamentalists don't like the Bible they've got!" You see, it is not very obedient to their definition of it.

For one thing, various accounts and statements in the Old Testament are pretty difficult to reconcile with the theology and ethics of the New Testament. John Bright[133] summarizes the problem:

> There is much in the Old Testament—and it ought frankly to be admitted—that offends the Christian's conscience. Its heroes are not always heroes, and are almost never saints. They lust, they brawl, and commit the grossest immorality; they plot, they kill, or seek to kill. And often enough their conduct receives no whisper of rebuke; it is just recorded. How are the stories of those things in any way a guide for the faith and conduct of the Christian? How shall he learn from them of the nature of his God and of the duty that his God requires of him? [. . .] Noble [the prophets] were and stirring their words, but did they not hate right well, and on occasion curse their enemies most heartily? And the psalms? Here is piety indeed, the most exalted and touching the world has ever known. But here is also that vengeful and wholly unforgiving spirit whose voice we hear in Psalm 109. Here is also that embittered exile who, in Psalm 137, spat out his hatred of his oppressors and wished that he might take their babies and dash their brains out against a rock. And many a troubled reader has asked how he can hear in such things the authoritative Word of God, how he can possibly receive them as a legitimate part of his supreme rule of faith and practice.

If the whole Bible is authoritative, what does one do with apparent contradictions such as these?

Bright mentions three classical "solutions." First, some deny that the Old Testament is really part of the Christian revelation at all. One would then throw out the Old Testament. Second, some would

---

133. John Bright, *The Authority of the Old Testament* (Grand Rapids: Baker Book House, 1975), pp. 55–56.

allegorize away any troublesome Old Testament passages until they obediently speak with the voice of the New Testament. With the resulting silence of the Old Testament's own voice, the practical effect is, again, to throw away the Old Testament. Thirdly, some propose that the Old Testament be sifted through the teaching of the New, the remaining material being considered authoritative. This, too, amounts to dispensing with the Old Testament, since it then would say nothing else or more than the New. Bright[134] points out that any value judgment to establish the authoritative element in Scripture will elevate the conscience of the individual to the real position of authority.

Once one comes to this point of realization there are two possibilities. The first is the way of forced harmonization. The exegete or theologian assumes that the Bible must teach the same basic doctrines and ethics throughout. Any "progressive revelation" supplements rather than displaces the old. With the exception of "cults" like the Worldwide Church of God, this approach is seldom followed consistently. For example, the New Testament undeniably calls a halt to certain aspects of the Law of Moses (even so, one often enough hears exhortations to tithing and "Sabbath" observance). Among orthodox exegetes who take this option, the results will be either a few insignificant modifications of the ethics of either testament in the light of the other, or just another form of Bright's third "solution," that of making the Old Testament speak with the voice of the New.

The other possibility is that of admitting the difficulties and trying to deal with them. The concept of progressive revelation comes in handy. Bernard Ramm[135] reasons as follows:

> There is a progression in Scripture and unless this principle . . . is recognized there can be no clear exegesis of Scripture. Progressive

---

134. Bright, *Authority of the Old Testament*, pp. 69, 79, 91, 96, 108.

135. Bernard Ramm, "Biblical Hermeneutics" in Ramm, et. al., *Hermeneutics* (Grand Rapids: Baker Book House, 1972), pp. 23–24.

revelation means that God takes man where he finds him and with whatever notions he has of God and ethical principles and seeks to lead him higher and higher. . . . It involves the enlargement of the idea of God, the purification of ethical ideals, the spiritualizing of worship.

Partisans of progressive revelation insist that the principle is implicit in Jesus' statement, "For your hardness of heart he wrote you this commandment" (Mark 10:5). Here, they say, is a theological principle allowing us to face the moral and theological difficulties of the Old Testament without leading to another form of Bright's third "solution." Since God has been revealing something of himself throughout salvation-history, there should appear throughout the Bible a consistent, but ever-deepening, stream. One still needs to "distill" this in the Old Testament, but the "canon within the canon" will be seen in the whole of the Bible, not just the New Testament. As Bright[136] puts it:

> If we are rightly to understand the Bible, we must . . . grasp the unifying structure of belief that undergirds it both in the Old Testament and in the New. [. . .] [B]iblical theology is an inductive, descriptive discipline that seeks through an examination of the biblical records to determine and set forth in its own terms the essential and normative content of the faith of the Old Testament and the New, respectively, as distinct . . . from transient, peripheral, aberrant, and incidental features within their own structures.

But is Bright perhaps contradicting himself when he says the following? "The attempt to isolate an authoritative element within Scripture by means of a value judgment leads inevitably to a breakdown of the whole concept of authority."[137] Bright sees no problem

---

136. Bright, *Authority of the Old Testament,* p. 125.

137. Bright, *Authority of the Old Testament,* p. 108.

here, because he seeks to let the Bible itself isolate the authoritative core. However, the principle stumbling block for many is the idea that there could be an authoritative "core" at all if the whole Bible is inspired. The problem arises from a particular understanding of the nature of the Bible as a book of Scripture. Although few evangelicals and fundamentalists still hold to the strictest dictation model of inspiration, most probably still presuppose a "magic book" model of Scripture. It is tacitly, even unconsciously, assumed that, like a systematic theology textbook, the Bible must have a reasonably clear answer to every important question. Because the apostle Paul wrote that "all scripture is God-breathed and is profitable for doctrine, reproof, correction, and instruction" (1 Tim. 3:16), and "all" must mean *all*, many Christians are inclined to look for theology and ethics in narrative, poetic, or other portions of the Bible where such is apparently neither intended nor present. If one will let the Bible speak for itself, many difficulties might disappear. Let us recognize that the Bible sometimes speaks non-postulationally. This realization should make "biblical theology" (as Bright defines it) less frightening to conservatives. Bernard Ramm[138] adds that the same sort of misunderstanding precipitates many of the Bible-science controversies: "The phenomena of scripture clearly militate against the notion that everything in the Bible is a revelation of 'wholly other,' perfect truth, dropped, as it were, from heaven."

Living on Borrowed Truth

The study of comparative religion reveals (at least) two very significant things to the evangelical theologian. First, he may be surprised to learn that certain aspects of the biblical revelation are distinctly paralleled in other religions. Second, he even finds notions and concepts original to other religions which appear later in the progress

---

138. Bernard Ramm, *The Christian View of Science and Scripture* (Grand Rapids: Eerdmans, 1974).

of biblical revelation. For instance, it seems that concepts of Satan, salvation, and eschatology which appeared first in Zoroastrianism came into Judaism, and then into the Bible, by way of the Babylonian Captivity.[139] The early stories of Genesis find parallels in other ancient Near-Eastern literature. Other similarities between ancient Israelite religion and that of her neighbors include the sacrificial system itself, the Jerusalem temple, the desert shrine, or tabernacle, the literature of psalms and proverbs, and the activity of charismatic prophets. Does any of this matter? If the Bible is divinely inspired, does it have to be unique in every way? Aquinas certainly didn't think so. Remember, he distinguished between *de novo* revelation and the inspired use of non-inspired source materials.

The Crisis of Protestant Literalism

Traditional Protestant approaches to Scripture are seriously problematical. Precisely how has the fortress of Protestant literalism crumbled? Protestant hermeneutics are based on Martin Luther's paradigm, the first axiom of which is *sola scriptura*, which means that scriptural interpretation is logically prior to theology or tradition. One should get one's beliefs from scripture, and not impose one's beliefs *on* it, as Luther's Catholic opponents did.

The second axiom asserts the normativeness of scripture's single, natural, literal sense. It must be read with the same methods one would use to decipher any other ancient writing. Thus Luther's espousal of the *grammatico-historical method*. One does exegesis of the Bible according to the historical information available on the times and according to the grammar of the Greek, Hebrew, and Aramaic languages. Just as one would never look for allegorical and kabbalistic secret meanings smuggled into Caesar's *Gallic Wars* by the Holy Spirit, neither should one so approach the Bible. Inspired though

---

139. Ninian Smart, *The Religious Experience of Mankind* (New York: Scribners, 1969), pp. 249, 292.

the Bible is, it is an inspired *human* writing, to be read by humans as humans read human writings! One needs no divine X-ray vision to discern what the scriptural authors intended to tell us. Even in the case of the Revelation of John, one does one's homework familiarizing oneself with the codes of the literary genre of apocalypses. Even puzzles are to be taken literally, i.e., strictly according to the known rules for deciphering them.

The inspiration of scripture is irrelevant during the process of exegesis. Where it becomes relevant is in the stage of hermeneutics, where we try to discern our obligation to do what scripture says, adjusting to our circumstances of today.

The third axiom of Protestant hermeneutics is the *Analogy of Scripture*. This is to assume the unity and harmony of the canonical books. If a book violates this "analogy," it is excluded from the canon. Thus Luther waxed bold to relegate Hebrews, James, Jude, and Revelation to an appendix to his New Testament canon, because he felt that they did not comport with the Pauline gospel of salvation by grace through faith alone. But within the canon, the prevailing maxim shall be that "scripture interprets scripture," the "less clear by the more clear." If, say, Paul is found seeming to say in one place that people will be saved by performing the works of the Law (Rom. 2:6–7, 13), we are to deem this text "less clear" than those in which he ("more clearly") says that no one will be saved by legal obedience (Rom. 3:20). The apparent sense of the former may seem clear in its own right. Its supposed lack of clarity comes from its seeming failure to match up with the apparent sense of the preferred texts. "Less clear" is thus seen to mean "apparently clear in meaning, but problematical in implication." The euphemism of "clarity" (or the lack of it) is, as we shall see, important since it masks an important equivocation.

The fourth axiom of Luther's paradigm is the *Perspicuity of Scripture*. We don't need an infallible interpreter, such as the Pope, since the infallible scripture is plain in its meaning to all sane, unprejudiced, and moderately intelligent readers. That may explain why Luther was scornful of those who disagreed with him: the Pope, Ulrich Zwingli, Kaspar Schwenkfeld, etc. He couldn't allow himself to believe they could rationally or sincerely disagree with him.

A House of Cards is Our Mighty Fortress

But, I am sorry to say, these four cardinal principles of Protestant hermeneutics contradict and devour one another, leaving biblicists with an incoherent mess. The assumption of the Analogy of Scripture is possible only insofar as we have already adopted the dogmatic presupposition of a single Divine Author of all parts of scripture ("plenary inspiration"). And then one feels one cannot read the Bible simply as any other set of texts. No one insists, for example, on harmonizing Calvin and Arminius! One does, of course, seek to iron out seeming contradictions between divergent passages in the work of a single author (St. Augustine, for example), but one does not refuse to admit as a last resort that the writer was inconsistent within a single work or may have changed his mind between one work and the next.

Even biblicists, so-called biblical literalists (though, as James Barr[140] points out, this is a misnomer, since literal interpretation is quickly sacrificed to non-literal so long as the latter is deemed more compatible with the supposed "inerrancy" of the biblical text) will admit that scripture is filled with "apparent contradictions." Apologist Gleason Archer even compiled an *Encyclopedia of Biblical Difficulties*, something one would hardly expect to be necessary with a perspicuous inerrant book, though the irony seems thus far to have escaped Archer and his readers. Biblicists feel they must deny that the Bible might contain "real" as opposed to "apparent" contradictions, because if it contained real ones, then biblicism ("The Bible

---

140. James Barr, *Fundamentalism* (Philadelphia: Westminster Press, 1978), p. 40.

says it; I believe it; that settles it!") would be sunk. If passage A con-
tradicted passage B, how would poor mortals know which biblical
text to believe and which to reject? Thus it seems better to hold that
the contradiction is merely apparent, that the solution to the puzzle
is merely elusive *thus far*. Somehow the seemingly clashing contents
of both texts could be shown to agree if we had some extra information. In the meantime we will just effectively ignore the scripture
passage that "apparently contradicts" the one which contains ideas
we want to believe, that our creed or church *tells* us to believe. Protestants will readily stake their eternal salvation on Romans 3:20 and
the doctrine of grace into which it neatly fits. What to do with Romans 2:6–7, 13? Ignore them, or, which is the same thing, pretend
they say what Romans 3:20 says.

How is it possible that biblicists have not yet grasped that "apparent" contradictions are absolutely fatal to their doctrine of "biblical
authority," based as it is on the "plain sense of the text"? Remember,
it is none other than the plain, straightforward, *apparent* sense of
the text that is authoritative for Protestants, that is, if we are to stick
with grammatico-historical exegesis and so fend off mischievous
Papistical allegorizing. That is what grammatico-historical exegesis
means: the apparent meaning. Luther framed this principle precisely
in order to rule out Catholic claims to have dug up some non-appar-
ent "real" meaning of the text. And yet it is just such a stratagem to
which inerrantists constantly repair with all their talk of "apparent
contradictions"! They are defending inerrancy in the same way medieval Catholics defended the sale of indulgences. Only in their case,
the irony is all the greater since the appeal to esoteric meanings of
scripture to defend desirable doctrines is an implicit repudiation of
the very hermeneutic on which all their other doctrinal beliefs rest!

If one doubts the truth of this, just look at the practical results
of the "apparent contradiction" or "more clear/less clear" subterfuge:
is not even the biblicist left deciding whether he will accept verse A
(e.g., Rom. 2:6–7, 13) as normative for faith and harmonize verse B

(e.g., Rom. 3:20) into pretended conformity with it? Or the other way around? Is Romans 3:20 to be seized on as the true teaching of God's Word, and Romans 2:6–7, 13 subordinated to it? This is exactly the same arbitrary procedure they fear would result if they were to admit that scripture "really" contradicts itself. The sole difference is whether one wants to *admit* one is setting aside the passage whose plain meaning one does not like.

But *is* the choice arbitrary? In one sense yes, since one might equally have chosen either text. In another sense, the choice is anything *but* arbitrary: it will be dictated by the needs of one's preferred or inherited theology. There is nothing arbitrary about that. Thus Walter Kaufmann[141] mocked that you can predict how a theologian will "gerrymander" the Bible as soon as you know what denominational label the theologian bears! And then what we are saying is that our doctrine is prior to our biblical exegesis and controls it before we ever even open the Bible. And that is the Roman Catholic view.

Moreover, the claim for the perspicuity of Scripture is demonstrably false, as witness the conflict of interpretations. Even if there were no contradictions or patent errors in scripture, the simple fact of ambiguity is enough to rule out "confident preaching of God's authoritative Word" as ridiculous and megalomaniacal.

Is There a "Plain Sense"?

Perhaps the problem in all this is the very notion that there is such a thing as the plain sense of the text, an unadorned, objective meaning that ought to be obvious to any unprejudiced reader. What if there just *is* no plain meaning, whether that of a doctrine one wants to embrace or that of a contradiction one would prefer to ignore?

With Stanley Fish,[142] guru of Reader Response criticism, we

---

141. Walter Kaufmann, *The Faith of a Heretic* (Garden City: Doubleday Anchor Books, 1963), p. 109.

142. Stanley Fish, *Is There a Text in This Class? The Authority of Interpre-*

must recognize that we belong to self-contained "communities of interpreters," sharing with our fellow members a set of assumptions as to what kind of thing to look for in texts, what methodology to use, and even what results we can expect. We are ultimately reading the text through a lens, feeding the text through a grinder of our own choosing. It will seem to us, secure within this "plausibility structure,"[143] that we are merely seeking the "plain sense" of the text, but it will seem so only because we naively take for granted a previously controversial reading that our community of interpreters has long ago come to take for granted. For medieval Catholics, some allegorical or anagogical reading that seems preposterous to us today seemed entirely natural, even inevitable. To them, Martin Luther's "truncated" reading of the "grammatico-historical" sense of the text seemed as crazy as it would seem to us if someone urged us to take the parables as straight historical anecdotes with no deeper meaning. Scripture is in the eye of the beholder.

This subjectivity is hidden from us by the fact that both our exegetical colleagues and opponents (the only ones we are close enough to, to argue with!) hold the same basic rules and assumptions we do. Within that common frame of mind we can have variations on a theme, but other communities of interpreters are forever sealed off from us. We are playing baseball; they are playing soccer. We can't play on the same field, much less win a victory over each other.

---

tive Communities (Cambridge: Harvard University Press, 1980).,

143. Berger and Luckmann, *Social Construction of Reality,* pp. 154–155.

14

The Miracle of the Supernatural
God's Technology

Thales of ancient Ionia probably qualifies as both the first scientist and the first philosopher. He invented science when he asked how the rain comes to fall. Religion (or myth) says rain is what happens when Zeus says, "Forsooth, let's have some rain here! Chop-chop!" Science, by contrast, tells us (or *hopes* to tell us) *how* it rains. Even if we still want to say it is the work of Father Zeus, there must be some *way*, some *method*, by which he does it, right? If his spoken word does the trick, *how*? Mustn't we picture some chain of cause and effect? If we picture Circe casting a spell, mustn't there be some *way* in which the spoken formula brings about the desired outcome? Doesn't there have to be, say, some kind of property in the "magic words"? The syllables have to set loose some vibrations that have an impact on the recipient of the curse, right? Like the radio: the sounds reach your speakers through the medium of radio waves. They don't just get there because somebody says they should. If you are just thinking that God says it and it happens, you are talking cartoons. The Koran says, "He saith unto a thing, 'Be!' and it is." But this presupposes that what is about to be created already exists to hear the divine command it must now obey. That paradox, I realize, is of-

161

fered to us, not hidden from us readers. It is clever and winsomely expressed, but it still does not make any sense. And that's fatal. That's my point: it just doesn't make any sense, even any *theological* sense.

Science fiction helps us see the theological relevance of this question. It is by now a common SF trope for alien visitors to display advanced technology that produces effects that seem supernatural and miraculous to us backwards earthlings. In some of these stories and movies the aliens seek to bamboozle us into regarding them as divine beings, angels, etc. Erich von Däniken's *Chariots of the Gods?* posits that religion on earth began in precisely this fashion. Though there is no proof of this, as far as I know, his theory is by no means absurd or out of the question. And there are modern UFO religions who believe that, e.g., Jesus' "miraculous" conception, without a human begetter, was artificial insemination by aliens, that his resurrection was like that of Klaatu in *The Day the Earth Stood Still* or Neelix on *Star Trek: Voyager*, i.e., mechanically induced. His ascension? "Beam me up, Scotty."

"So what?" you say? Simply that these fictions indicate how the traditional line between "natural" and "supernatural" may be erased. If "God" is not Being-itself, but rather *a* being among others, even the Supreme one, who thinks, plans, and acts with means to meet goals he has set, then his "miracles" are in effect futuristic medicine and technology, though techniques so far beyond ours that those terms aren't really appropriate anymore. But he, and his powers, would not be "supernatural," would they? He'd be more like Galactus or Thanos.

"Naturalistic Presuppositions"?

Christian apologists love to banish all critical readings of biblical miracle stories that take them as myths and legends. This they do by claiming that, despite good evidence, "liberal" critics like Bultmann first *presuppose* that miracles *never* happen and thus *did* not happen in the cases the Bible "records." The critical judgments, apologists insist, are purely deductive, circular, even bigoted. Here is a prime case of what Freud dubbed "reaction formation," the refusal or inability to recognize one's fault and the tendency instead to project it onto someone else.

Does it take a blanket presupposition for a historian to discount some miracle stories as legendary? No, because, as even Bultmann recognized, there is no problem accepting reports even of extraordinary things that we can still verify as occurring today, like faith healings and exorcisms. However you may wish to account for them, you can go to certain meetings and see scenes somewhat resembling those in the gospels. So it is by no means a matter of rejecting all miracle stories on principle. Biblical critics are not like the Committee for Scientific Investigation of Claims of the Paranormal. But a selective, piecemeal, and probabilistic acceptance of miracle stories is not what apologists want. They take umbrage that critics do not wind up accepting *any and all* biblical miracles. Otherwise how are we to understand the constant refrain that it is inconsistent for critics to strain out the gnat of the virgin birth while swallowing the resurrection?

So if it would not require a blanket principle to *reject* the historicity of particular miracle stories, we must ask if it would take a blanket principle to *require acceptance* of all biblical miracle stories. Clearly it would. And that principle cannot be simple supernaturalism, openness to the possibility of miracles. One can believe God capable of anything without believing that he did everything anybody may say he did. One can believe in the possibility of miracles without believing that every reported miracle must in fact have happened. No, the requisite principle is that of biblical inerrancy, the belief that all biblical narratives are historically accurate simply because they appear in the Bible. After all, it will not greatly upset William Lane Craig any more than it upset Warfield[144] to deny the historical accu-

---

144. Benjamin B. Warfield, *Counterfeit Miracles: A Defense of Divine Miracles Against Pagan, Medieval, and Modern Marvels* (New York: Scribners,

racy of medieval reports of miracles wrought by the Virgin Mary or by the sacramental wafer, much less stories of miracles wrought by Gautama Buddha or Apollonius of Tyana.

"Supernaturalism" is not at all the issue here. The issue is whether the historian is to abdicate his role as a sifter of evidence by accepting the dogma of inerrancy. Does fire become better fire when doused with water? That is what Craig wants, because he is trying to win souls for evangelicalism.

Nor is "naturalism" the issue when the historian employs the principle of analogy. As F.H. Bradley showed in *The Presuppositions of Critical History*,[145] no historical inference is possible unless the historian assumes a basic analogy of past experience with present. If we do not grant this, nothing will seem amiss in believing reports that A turned into a werewolf or that B changed lead into gold. "Hey, just because we don't see it happening today doesn't prove it never did!" One could as easily accept the historicity of Jack and the Beanstalk on the same basis, as long as one's sole criterion of historical probability is "anything goes!"

If there are Buddhist legends or Pythagorean tales about people walking on water but there is no present-day instance, is the historian to be maligned as a narrow dogmatist and, worse, a moral coward refusing to repent, if he or she judges the report of Jesus walking on the water to be an edifying legend, too?

The historical axiom of analogy does not dogmatize; critical historians are not engaging in metaphysical epistemology as if they could hop into a time machine and pontificate "A didn't happen! B did!" Again, William Lane Craig, N.T. Wright, and their brethren are just projecting. It is they, and not critical historians, who want to be able to point to sure results. Imagine the creed: "If thou shalt confess with thy mouth the Lord Jesus and believe in thy heart that

1918).

145. F.H. Bradley, *The Presuppositions of Critical History* (Chicago: Quadrangle Books, 1968).

God hath *probably* raised him from the dead, thou shalt *most likely* be saved." But who is the joke on here? Historians don't *have* creeds. They frame hypotheses. Sure, you can find some hidebound prof, some small-minded, insecure windbag who will not budge from a pet theory because he has too much personally invested in it. But you have no trouble recognizing such a person as a hack, a fake, a bad historian who ought to know better. The last thing you do is emulate such behavior and make it into an operating principle. But apologists do. Again, it's projection.

15

Hell with the Lid Off
We Have Such Sights to Show You!

Various Hebrew and Greek words are translated "hell" in the King James Bible. "Hell" itself comes from an old English word meaning "covered place" or "cover," as when they used to speak of "helling" instead of "peeling" potatoes. But are the history and evolution of the concept of Hell themselves covered by popular religious ignorance? I fear it is so. So my next task is to present, as Marjoe Gortner once titled a sermon, "Hell with the Lid Off."

Sheol refers to the Old Testament netherworld, derived from or shared with Babylonian religion. Sheol was pictured as a great walled city with barred gates, a place of dust and shadows from which one could never hope to return. So Enkidu, on his deathbed, describes it to Gilgamesh. There the "shades" (*rephaim*) of the dead shuffle about in a confused stupor forever. No one praises God there, nor does God spare the place a thought (Psalm 88:2–10). It is much like the Greek Hades, where people pass a dreary eternity.

Hades is borrowed from Greek religion, denoting the subterranean place of the dead, pretty much equivalent to Sheol, kind of a dimly lit parking lot for the souls/shades of the dead. The shade of Achilles told his old friend Odysseus that he would sooner be a slave on earth than the king of "this place." Hades is a place of torment in Luke 16:23 but apparently just denotes the mortuary existence of Sheol in Matthew 11:23, where the reference is to Isaiah 14's picture of a dreary but not particularly horrific Sheol.

Tartaros is something worse. Eventually the Greek Hades had been divided into a place of reward (the Elysian Fields) and of punishment (Tartaros). Uranos had long ago confined his monstrous children, the Giants—including Gyges, or Gog (Ezek. 38:2, 3, 14,16, 18, etc.)—and the Hundred-handed there, just as God consigns his fallen Sons (Gen. 6:1–4) underground in Jude 6 and 2 Peter 2:4. Tartaros as a cavern-world of fiery jets and streams of boiling water is a piece of mythical geography derived from the volcanic springs and lava pits of Sicily. The idea was passed on into Judaism, Christianity, and Islam by means of the influence of Sicilian and Italian Pythagoreanism.[146]

Gehenna means "the Valley of the Sons of Hinnom." It is also called Tophet, which thus became a synonym for Hell. Tophet was believed to be the gateway to the subterranean volcanic realm of the god Moloch/Molech,[147] who received child sacrifices there. (See 2 Kgs. 23:10; Jer. 7:31; 19:6, 11–13.) Originally, however, Molech's realm was not a place of torment for the wicked. The sacrificed babies were simply snacks for the horrible deity.

Hellish Hypotheses

The majority view of historic Christianity is Hell as *eternal punishment* (Rev. 14:9–11; Matt.13:49–50; 25:41, 46). The notion of degrees of punishment within Hell, so important in Dante's *Inferno*, occurs

---

146. Peter Kingsley, *Ancient Philosophy, Mystery, and Magic: Empedocles and Pythagorean Tradition* (New York: Oxford University Press, 1995), p. 193.

147. John Day, *Molech: A God of Human Sacrifice in the Old Testament.* University of Cambridge Oriental Publications (Cambridge: Cambridge University Press, 1990).

in Luke 12:47–48 and explicitly in the Apocalypse of Peter, a text once widely read in Palestinian churches on Good Friday.

Some believe Hell is millions of years of torment, ending in *annihilation*. This was the teaching of William Marrion Branham, Pentecostal faith healer. He still has followers today (who accord him messianic standing, so he ought to know, one supposes), many years after his passing, and they keep the doctrine alive. This version preserves the biblical meaning of "eternal" as "till the end of the age," or "through the ages." Similarly, the early Universalist Charles Chauncey[148] suggested an aeons-long Hell that could give way to salvation if the sufferer repented.

Jehovah's Witnesses, nearly a world religion in their own right, believe in the *annihilation of the wicked* in the Lake of Fire after the final resurrection of the dead. A reexamination of his father's hellfire preaching began the theological thinking of Charles Taze Russell, founder of the Jehovah's Witnesses sect. Matthew 10:28 might be interpreted this way. This is the view of Herbert W. Armstrong's Worldwide Church of God as well.

According to the doctrine of *conditional immortality*[149] the wicked just remain dead. It is the belief of Seventh Day Adventists, who may appeal on its behalf to Isaiah 26:14, 19 and 1 Thessalonians 4:13–14.

Hell may also be understood as a *purgatory*, where you atone for your own sins, with no reference to the atonement of Christ. It is of finite duration: you will get out once you have paid the last farthing. Hell as a purgatory is the view of Buddhists, Hindus, and Zoroastrians. No eternal Hell for them! It lasts only for untold millions of

148. Charles Chauncey, *The Mystery Hidden from Ages and Generations, Made Manifest by the Gospel-Revelation: Or, The Salvation of All Men. The Grand Thing Aimed at in the Scheme of God, As Opened in the New Testament Writings, and Entrusted with Jesus Christ to Bring into Effect.* (1784, rpt. Arno Press & The New Yorl Times, 1969).

149. Norman T. Burns, *Christian Mortalism from Tyndale to Milton* (Cambridge: Harvard University Press, 1972).

years! Matthew 5:26; 18:34–35 may be read as referring to a "limited liability" Hell. It warns of the danger of being sent to debtors' prison, but is this simple prudential advice? Or is it, as seems likely, a metaphor for postmortem dangers? If the latter, it presupposes a strict calculus of sins. Father Guido Sarducci represents this view when he speaks of "thirty-five cent sins." Remember," he warns, "They mount up!"

Many theologians, flinching at the notion of endless torment inflicted by a "merciful" God, like to redefine Hell as exclusion from the presence of God. (Would that reduce Hell to Limbo?) Hell is understood here not as physical pain but as emotional regret, frustration, remorse—at not being able to bask in God's presence. (This is the favorite have-your-cake-and-eat-it-too solution of conservatives who do not want to *say* they reject Hell-belief but do anyway. It is a twin to the lame Moral Influence Theory of the atonement in being more of a sentiment than a doctrine. After all, the absence of God is just the thing the sinner always liked best, right? Experiencing it for eternity ought to be heaven! As Kant pointed out, it's only the righteous who repents, not the sinner, who has no regrets! In fact, this is not coincidentally the very doctrine held by the irreligious when they say, "Hell? I won't mind it! It'll just be a big party with my friends!"

And it hardly makes God look less cruel: if sinners in Hell *have* finally come to pine for God, doesn't that mean they have repented? And then we must imagine God chuckling maliciously at the irony of it: "Too late, you poor bastards!"

Burning Questions

Does the sinner *choose Hell* by not choosing God? Or isn't Hell always described in the New Testament as a punishment *extrinsically imposed* by God in judgment? There are plenty of pains that we should have seen coming, that we invited anyway, as the natural repercussions of our actions. But this is like saying the murderer killed so that he could be executed. Besides, there would have to be a lot more compelling evidence that there *is* a Hell for a sinner to be imagined as holding it before himself as one of the options on *Let's Make a Deal*. The whole thing is simply a pathetic attempt to get a sadistic God off the hook. Sadly, C.S. Lewis favored this nonsense.[150]

Is Hell a deterrent? If so, it doesn't seem to be working very well, since most felons in jail and on death row are believers whose faith didn't deter them. There are very few agnostics, atheists or Universalists in the Big House. Besides, as Kant pointed out, to make a threat (or a reward!) the basis for morality is to poison the well of moral motivation. As Erik Erikson would say, "Turn or burn" exhortations only ensure that the poor, intimidated hearer remains at the most retarded, childish stage of moral maturity. *"Gimme any confession you want and I'll sign it! Just don't torture me!"* What, God is like the North Koreans?

Is Hell hot? It is in Revelation 14:9–11 (at least for the poor wretches who swore fealty to the Beast to get their green card) and in Matthew 25:41. Buddhism offers quite the diversity of infernal options at different temperatures! Try one on for size, won't you? There are *Eight Hot Hells*, each with four ante-hells (cf., Lovecraft: "the antechamber of Hell").[151] They also have subcompartment Hells, listed here, just to give you the full effect.[152]

> Reanimation Hell: after being torn apart, your members are joined again for another go at it—forever!
> Sewage Hell
> Sword Circle (with hell-spark "cluster bombs")
> Cooking Pot Hell

---

150. C.S. Lewis, *The Problem of Pain* (New York: Macmillan, 1962), p. 127.

151. H.P. Lovecraft, "The Rats in the Walls."

152. See Daigan and Alicia Matsunga, *The Buddhist Concept of Hell* (New York: Philosophical Library, 1972):

Hell of Many Pains (taking whatever you dished out)

Smothering Darkness Hell

Torment by Cries of Fowls

Over the Cliff Hell

Disease Hell

Iron-paired Hell

Evil Stick Hell

Black Weasel Hell

Spinning Hell

Hell of Complete Pain

Red Lotus Hell

Pond Hell

Hell of Torments Received in the Air

Black Line Hell: one's body is marked with black lines along which red-hot saws begin to rip.

Equal Screaming Hell (where no one hears)

Eye-plucking Hell

Fearful Vulture Hell

Squeezing and Grinding (or Crowded) Hell

Stabbing, Cooking, Boiling Hell

Shredding Hell

Veins-Cutting Hell

Hell of Evil Sights

Frustrated Bestiality Hell

Fiery Rapist Gay Hell

Hell of Enduring Pain

Insect Hell

"Tantalus Hell"

Hell of Burning Tears

Hell Where All Organs Are Destroyed

Hell of No Other Shore

Deadly Lotus Pond Hell

Molten Copper Hell

Fire-Jar Hell

Hell of Fiery Iron Powder

Screaming Hell (scalding water poured down your throat!)

Great Howling Hell

Hell Filled with Voices

Burning Hair Hell

Fire Insect Hell

Burning Steel Pestle Hell

Twin Flame of Burning Stones

Slaughtering Hell

Field of Steel Trees

Hell of Complete Darkness

Field of Yama-ruja (demons burn you, head to sole)

Sword Forest

Large Sword Forest

Plantain Smoke Forest

Forest of Burning Smoke

Burning Cloud Mist Hell

Random Demonic Harassment Hell

Great Screaming Hell (you're simmered in molten lead!)

Roaring Hell

Hell of Infinite Numbers of Pains

Hell of Unbearable Pain

Hell of Hatred

Hell of Total Darkness

Dark Smoke Hell

Hell Where Sinners Drop Like Flies

Dismemberment by Burning in Blue Lotus Flames Hell

Rolling Hell (hindered from protecting endangered loved ones)

Hell of Vain Desires

Twin Suffering Hell

Hell Where Enemies clip off your flesh and force you to eat it.

Hell of Diamond-Beaked Birds

Flaming Hair Hell

Stabbing Pain Hell

Hell of Limitless Pain

Hell Where Blood and Bones are Consumed

Red Hot Hell

Fire Sixteen Times as Hot as any other Hell

Paradise-Mirage Charcoal Pit Hell

Circling Dragon Hell

Molten Copper, Iron Fish, and Diamond-beaked Worms Hell

Iron Cauldron Hell

Floating in a River of Blood Hell

Bone-eating Insect Hell

Seeing Loved Ones Cooked Hell

Endless Submersion Hell

Lotus with Diamond Thorns Hell

Dangerous Cliff Hell

Diamond Bone Hell

Black Line Hell

Crocodile Hell

Dark Fire Wind Hell

Diamond Beak Hornet Hell

White Hot Hell

Hell Burning in All Directions

Fearful Hell of Large Roaring Bodies

Burning Hell of String-Like Worms

Fire Rain Hell (diamond-sand grinds the flesh from the body)

Place of Internal Boiling

Shouting Hell

Demonic Skin-Peeling Hell

Hell of Raining Iron Spikes

Hell of Marrow-Sucking Worms

Flesh-scraping Hell

Flaming Arrow and Diamond Sword Net Hell

Cooking Pot Hell

Thousand-headed Dragon Hell

Cooking and Pulverizing Hell

Hell of Spinning Trees and Molten Pewter

Relentless Hell

Bird Mouth Hell: one hundred times the pain of the previous seven, as one's mouth is ripped away (as the hunter tears away the bird's beak), grows back, gets ripped away again, etc.

Hell Where Everything Faces the Ground

Genital Torture Hell

Hell of Roaring Beasts

Hell of Being Devoured by Iron Beasts

Hell of Black Bile

Ocean of Corpses Hell

Nightmare Hell

Hell of Crushing Beneath the Root of a Burning Tree

Hell of Crushing by Mountains

Hell of Dropping by a Giant Bird

Hell of Sparks

Hell of Blinding by Molten Copper or Hot Sand

Hell of Stench

Hell of Iron Plates

Hell of Eleven Flames:

But there are also Eight Cold Hells! Bring your long johns!

Chapping Hell: repeated dips in freezing water

Popped Blister Hell

Inarticulate Cry Hell

Paralyzed Tongue Hell

Teeth-Gnashing Hell

Blue Flower Sores Hell

Inflamed Sores Hell

Flesh-Dropping Frostbite Hell

Besides these, there are some 84,000 local hells situated here and there in remote places on earth, in mountains, lakes, etc. Plus a kind of No-Man's Land Hell of rotting corpses, sewage, etc., which one must cross (without a map) should one get the chance to escape Hell once one has done one's time. There is something like this in the Nag Hammadi text The Book of Thomas the Contender. The fantastic variety of Buddhist Hells is echoed in Christian Hell-texts from the

Apocalypse of Peter on through Dante. Each Hell is fit penance for various categories of sinners.[153]

These surreal horrors bring to mind the words of 1 Corinthians 15:50, "I tell you this, brethren: flesh and blood cannot inherit the kingdom of God." The same holds true for the kingdom of Hell, doesn't it? I'm not talking about physical bodies, but rather human psyches. Imagine the limitations of the flesh were dropped away. Imagine there was no prospect of death to give perspective on life. Here is another of those places where features of historic Christianity, when consistently extrapolated, seem to be revealed as something more like Hinduism or Buddhism. Schleiermacher[154] admitted that an immortal, heavenly existence must be so different from earthly life that it remains unimaginable this side of the grave. First Corinthians 13:12 had long before said the same: "For now we see in a mirror dimly, but then face to face. Now I know in part; then I shall know fully, even as I have been fully known." Now try to imagine an *eternity* of overwhelming torment. Could the human psyche endure that without escaping into insanity?

Hellocaust

These days everyone seems to be pausing to observe with appropriate gravity one of the most chilling of recent historical events: the Holocaust. Which one?, you might ask. In Woody Allen's film *Hannah and her Sisters*, Frederick the moody intellectual remarks that for the first time in months or years he has spent an evening watching TV. Among the flickering spectacles he beheld was yet another panel of pundits talking about Hitler's extermination of six million

---

153. L. Austine Waddell, *Tibetan Buddhism, With Its Mystic Cults, Symbolism, and Mythology* (New York: Dover Publications, 1972 [orig., 1895 as *The Buddhism of Tibet, Or Lamaism.*]), pp. 90–98; Daigan and Alicia Matsunaga, *The Buddhist Concept of Hell* (New York: Philosophical Library, 1972), pp. 75–106.

154. Schleiermacher, *Christian Faith*, pp. 717–720.

Jews. All the intellectuals confessed themselves baffled as to how it could have happened. Not Frederick. "What they should be asking themselves is, given human nature, why isn't it happening all the time?" And of course it is.

Christians take the Holocaust seriously in part, I suspect, as a token way of atoning for the awful guilt born by their religion in fanning the flames of anti-Jewish persecutions over the centuries. Certainly Martin Luther, to whom we owe the doctrine of the soul's justification by grace through faith alone (I am not sure the doctrine ever crossed the mind of the apostle Paul in that form)—Luther, I say, was an anti-Semitic devil who urged his fellow justified sinners to torch synagogues and burn the Talmud.

Christians look back on such blemishes on the history of their faith and reflect that it would indeed have been better to suffer such persecution than to inflict it. Hence their eagerness to pause and ponder the Holocaust. But their apparent sensitivity rings hollow to me. For the astonishing fact is that Christians by and large have repudiated very little after all. For most of them still believe that God intends to persecute Jews to a degree far more horrifying than Hitler ever thought of doing. Many still believe that for the simple fact of being Jews, that is, not being Christians, Jews will be shipped off by the trainloads to the ovens of Hell. They believe this to be the will and plan of God and that furthermore, as good Christians, they must themselves second God's will with their own assent.

Whenever I happen to see the image of Adolf Hitler on TV and my daughters are with me, I always tell them that is Adolf Hitler, and that he was the most evil man who ever lived. And yet I doubt that even Hitler's diabolical brain ever contemplated doing to Jews what pious Christians have slated for them: a never-ending torture such as no earthly Inquisitor could inflict.

If you believe the orthodox Christian doctrine of Hell and of who is destined to go there, I ask you to own up to the sobering implications of this thing you believe. Picture the scene, will you? God, supposedly the merciful father of the human race, is planning to exile millions of souls to eternal torture for their failure to embrace a particular religious creed.

In fact, the Southern Baptist Convention has figured out how many Americans, state by state, are headed for Hell. This seems to them a simple matter of demographics, not to say demongraphics. All they have to do is to look at the church membership statistics county by county, town by town. Because to them it is clear that Jews, Unitarians, Catholics, secularists, Hindus, Mormons, Muslims, Buddhists are all damned. The arrogance of this, which is all intended quite straight-facedly, needs no comment. Why do the Southern Baptists imagine that all these folks deserve Hell? I cannot imagine that anybody deserves Hell, not even Hitler. Can any mortal have done anything to merit *eternal torture*? Think of what you are saying!

What sort of a God could even consider torturing people for eternity? What cruelty, what sadism! "The smoke of their torment goes up for ever and ever; and they have no rest, day and night." That's the way the Bible puts it. Is that what you believe? The God who could engineer such a thing would be a devil. And those who worship him with eyes wide open would qualify as diabolists.

Worse yet, it has defined its god, its moral ideal ("Be ye therefore perfect even as your Father in heaven is perfect," Matt. 5:48), as being capable of unthinkable cruelty, thus establishing a precedent for their own possible deeds. "If my God hates those who hate him, I ought to do as my God does, and I will hate them too."[155]

As it happens, I doubt that many traditionalist believers in these abhorrent doctrines have embraced the implications of what they say they believe. Alan Watts,[156] an Episcopalian priest turned Zen Buddhist, put it well:

---

155. Ballou, *Treatise on Atonement*, p. 55.

156. Alan Watts, *Beyond Theology: The Art of Godmanship* (New York: World Publishing Company, 1971), p. 83.

It is quite obvious to the canny observer that most Christians, including clergy and devout laity, do not believe in Christianity. If they did, they would be screaming in the streets, taking daily full-page advertisements in the newspapers, and subscribing for the most hair-raising television programs every night of the week. Even Jehovah's Witnesses are polite and genteel in their door-to-door propaganda. Nobody, save perhaps a few obscure fanatics, is really bothered by the idea that . . . most people are sinners and unbelievers, and will probably go to hell. So what? Let God worry about that one!

Watts is right: most Christians have never faced the implications of the rhetoric they use. At least I hope they haven't. Because as Rousseau said, you can't live at peace with those you have condemned to Hell.

How terrible to hear some self-appointed middle-class, coffee-clatch evangelist telling people glibly that they are going to spend eternity in the flames. Poor fools, they only prove out Wilfred Cantwell Smith's dictum: "except at the cost of insensitivity or delinquence, it is morally not possible actually to go out into the world and say to devout, intelligent, fellow human beings: 'We are saved and you are damned.'"[157]

Why does this medieval doctrine continue to claim a place in Christian theology? To put it plainly, if to rationalize the tragic death of Jesus you decide he must have died to save the human race, then there must be something sufficiently serious that they need saving *from*.

I know, there are theological reasons for Hell. God is too holy to sweep sin under the rug. He *has* to deal with it. Christ's death is the only remedy, since his life is the only one that could be a fit payment, short of the rest of us going to Hell. So if we fail to believe in him as

---

157. Wilfred Cantwell Smith, *The Faith of Other Men*. A Mentor Book (New York: New American Library, 1965), p. 119.

the savior, there is no alternative. To Hell with us! I admit, it does make an ominous kind of sense.

But as Wilfred Cantwell Smith[158] said, "The damnation of my neighbor is too weighty a matter to rest on a syllogism." In other words, if the doctrine of the atonement logically requires that most people are going to be tortured day and night for ever and ever, then that means the doctrine of the atonement is a *reductio ad absurdum*. That is, precisely by taking it to its last logical consequence, you reveal the idea to have been wrong-headed to begin with. If that's the way it ends up, then for Christ's sake, it has to be a false doctrine!

And that's not all. The doctrine, tolerating and implicitly defending the divine willingness to torture, is degrading to the one who holds it. If you do take it seriously, look what will happen to you, or what *has* happened to you: you are willing to redefine morality to include torturing people in a worse way than Hitler ever did.

Don't you think your theology has any impact on your soul? What happens to you if you redefine God as essentially cruel and fascistic? Insofar as you take your religion seriously, you make yourself over in the image of your God. And if your God is a torturer and a bigot, you will become a cruel bigot, too. Such faith corrupts the soul until, as the Epistle to Titus says, one's conscience is seared, its nerves deadened.

I know one thing from the New Testament. If the gospel means anything at all, it has to mean this: "The Son of Man came to save men's lives, not to destroy them." But the belief in a Hell stoked for non-Christians means that Christ came into the world to provide an occasion for most of humanity to be damned to Hell! And if that is what you think he came to do, then you know not what spirit you are of, for "God sent his Son not to condemn the world, but that the world through him might be saved"!

Do you believe in Jesus the savior or Jesus the destroyer? The

---

158. Smith, *Faith of Other Men*, p. 123.

destroyer of those who do not share your beliefs? Isn't that what the traditional doctrine amounts to? But I tell you, Jesus the destroyer is the Antichrist. That's exactly what Jews always thought as Christians persecuted them in the name of Jesus. You're not saying they were right, are you?

I have already discounted the ludicrous notion that sinners and unbelievers actually *choose* to go to hell. Nobody (pointedly, not God) forces them against their will. So says C.S. Lewis:

> There are only two kinds of people in the end: those who say to God, "Thy will be done," and those to whom God says, in the end, "Thy will be done." All that are in Hell, choose it. Without that self-choice there could be no Hell.[159]

No, anyone can see through that absurd ruse. The logic of the thing is clear: God sends them to Hell against their will, just as the earthly justice system imprisons convicted criminals against their will. So I ask, if God is going to overrule the sinner's will by damning them, why doesn't he just *sanctify* the bastards? They probably wouldn't want that either, but it sure beats having your intestines roasted on a spit in Hell forever.

Hellophobia

Finally, there are four things that make me dismiss the notion as not plausible enough to worry about. First, there is the implied notion of a "loving" God willing to torment people forever. This is just nonsense, even for fiends like Hitler. Such a God *is* Hitler. And if the criterion is passing a theology exam—it's just so absurd.

Second, we can trace the gradual evolution of the Hell concept. The Old Testament knows nothing of it, instead positing either just plain death; or the Babylonian shadow realm of Sheol to which all

---

159. C.S. Lewis, *The Great Divorce* (New York: Macmillan, 1946), p. 72.

must go, good or evil; or the borrowed Hades and Tartaros of the Greeks, ultimately based on the volcanic geography of Sicily. The truth does not grow in such a fashion. Myths do.

Third, if one fears reprisals for not buying Christianity, what the heck? By accepting it, you are *ipso facto* buying a ticket to one or more Islamic, Buddhist, Hindu Hells! If you're going to be afraid of Hell, there's no escape that way! The religions you *didn't* accept might be right, and you're headed for *their* infernos!

Fourth, the whole idea retards moral growth by making it impossible for the Hell believer ever to grow beyond the crudest, most infantile "morality." "Keep your hand out of the cookie jar, or mommy's going to spank you!" A doctrine that retards moral growth simply cannot be taken seriously, any more than one that promotes bigotry. We just cannot cripple ourselves by disregarding our better judgment and basing our beliefs on fear, fear of Hell.

The recurring worry, "But what if Hell *is* real?" must be recognized for what it is: what we as Christians called a temptation: an insidious whispering voice bidding us do the wrong thing. We must stand our ground and refuse to give in! Only so can we ever arrive at "a spirit of power, love, and a sound mind." The voices will die away after a while. There is no reason to take them seriously, and we must ever remind ourselves of that.

16

No-show Second Coming

Keep Watching the Skies!

Hermann Samuel Reimarus,[160] an eighteenth-century Deist, wrote a scathing and insightful critique of Christianity and the Bible. One of his most powerful points, in my estimation, was this: of all Jesus' ostensible revelations of heavenly secrets, the only one testable on this side of the morgue was the prediction of the Parousia within the very generation of Jesus and his contemporaries. Will you go to heaven one day? You'll have to wait to find out, won't you? Is there a loving heavenly Father watching over you? The evidence is admittedly equivocal, which is why you have to have faith that it is so. But the Parousia prediction is pretty cut-and-dried. "Every eye shall see him." But *nada*. Nothing happened. How is Christianity to recover from *that*? And the implications are fatal: if Jesus' "revelation" on this topic was false, why believe anything else that he "revealed"?[161]

---

160. Hermann Samuel Reimarus, *Reimarus: Fragments.* Trans. Ralph S. Fraser. Lives of Jesus Series. Charles H. Talbert, ed. (Philadelphia: Fortress Press, 1970), pp. 227–228.

161. An excruciatingly meticulous, also fresh and humorous, treatment of the delay of the Parousia and the apologists' many cringe-worthy evasions may be found in Mark Smith, *Broken Promises: Jesus & The Second Coming* (Amazon Kindle, 2020).

What was it George Santyana said?

Those who cannot learn from history are doomed to repeat it. Those who do not remember their past are condemned to repeat their mistakes. Those who do not read history are doomed to repeat it. Those who fail to learn from the mistakes of their predecessors are destined to repeat them. Those who do not know history's mistakes are doomed to repeat them.

That is exactly the case with this steadfastly ignored lesson. Having rationalized the failure of the Parousia, the early Christians bequeathed to their posterity a neurosis of repression of the Great Trauma, and every new Christian generation has repeated the error. All have believed that Christ will sooner or later return, but some groups in every one of those generations have announced the coming to occur in their own day, and, like clockwork, those predictions failed, too, just like the original.

This bizarre history of repeated expectation and repeated disappointment reminds me of a great *Saturday Night Live* skit from, I think, the 1980s. Kevin Nealon plays the dad in a family gathered round the Christmas tree on Christmas morning. There are no presents under the tree. The police are there, thinking the gifts have been stolen. But it is not so. Dad tries to comfort his children: "Well, kids, I guess we just weren't good enough again this year. But we'll just try extra hard next year, and maybe Santa will reward us with presents *next* Christmas!" The puzzled police officers begin to grasp that the dad still believes in Santa Claus and depends upon the jolly old elf to supply the presents! This might as well be a parable about Christians stubbornly believing that Jesus will soon return in his sleigh with eight tiny reindeer, even though it never happens.

Popular American eschatology (= the doctrine of the Last Things) constitutes the game they play while they wait. There are endless debates over how to juggle three items: the Rapture (Greek for "catching up"), the Great Tribulation, and the Millennium. The various positions can be set out according to how they arrange these features. Most fundamentalists advocate *Pre-Millennialism*: After the Second Coming of Christ, he will reign on earth with the resurrected righteous for a literal period of one thousand years. Wicked survivors of Armageddon, along with their descendants, will populate the earth during this time, at the end of which Satan will escape his confinement in the Abyss and lead the wicked nations ("Gog and Magog") in a final assault on Jerusalem, where Jesus reigns. This attempt will fail, and the wicked dead of all ages will be raised to be judged and cast into the Lake of Fire. Then the earth will be regenerated/recreated. (It is worth noting that Revelation 20:4 seems to picture only the martyrs of the Beast, beheaded during the Tribulation, as resurrected at the commencement of the Millennium, with the rest of the righteous of past ages rising together with the wicked at the close of the Millennium.) Most church fathers before Augustine who mentioned it seem to have been Pre-Millennialists.

Pre-Tribulationism is the most popular version of Pre-Millennialism.[162] It was the brainchild, as far as we know, of Edward Irving, founder of the Catholic Apostolic Church, and John Nelson Darby, founder of the Plymouth Brethren and of Dispensationalist theology, both in the 1820s. The idea is that believers will be caught up to heaven in a "secret rapture," a kind of preliminary Second Coming where Christ comes not to earth to rule, but only within shouting distance to wake the righteous dead. These then return with him to heaven for the duration of a seven-year Tribulation. This view is derived primarily from Dispensationalist ecclesiology (= Doctrine of the Church), which regards the Christian Church and Jewry as two separate covenant peoples, each with its own distinct role in God's plan. The Tribulation (or "Time of Jacob's Trouble") is solely intended to chastise Jews for their unbelief in Jesus Christ. Christians have

---

162. John Walvoord, *The Rapture Question* (Grand Rapids: Zondervan Academic, rev. ed., 1978).

nothing to do with this, so Darby reasoned that they must be literally extracted from the planet while it is going on, lest it strike them, too.

Exegetically, the only ground of appeal for Pre-Tribulationism is to those texts which warn the reader to be on the watch, since the coming of Christ could happen at any moment (Matt. 24:42–25:13). However, this only has force if one imagines that all New Testament writers shared the expectation of a seven-year Tribulation, the idea being that, if the Tribulation hadn't started yet, you'd know the Second Coming must be at least seven years away, not imminent, unless the Rapture was to take place *before* the Tribulation. But some New Testament writers never mention any seven-year duration. On the other hand, some do warn their readers that they will not see the Second Coming until certain events have transpired, such as the emergence of the Man of Sin, etc. (2 Thes. 2:1), so they cannot very well have thought the Second Coming (or Parousia) was imminent.

Mid-Tribulationism is a variant of Pre-Tribulationism, the difference being that since only the second half of the reign of the Antichrist (Dan. 9:27) is to be a persecution of the Jews, Christians might as well hang around till the fur starts to fly!

Partial Rapturism is another variation on Pre-Tribulationism, whereby only those in a sanctified state will be caught up in the Rapture. Backsliders will have to endure the Great Tribulation, which will serve to purify them. They will finally be raptured/resurrected at the end of the Tribulation. Luke 21:34–36 and Revelation 3:10 do seem to hold out the prospect that some faithful disciples will be exempted from the Tribulation, even though others, also genuine Christians but lazy ones, will have to undergo it. Matthew 24:45–51 and 25:1–13 seem simply to threaten the unready with damnation, but if one believed in eternal security, those verses might be taken as further evidence of a Partial Rapture.

Post-Tribulationism is the oldest version of Pre-Millenarianism. It locates the Tribulation before the Millennium, but the Rapture comes *after* the Tribulation (Matt. 24:29–31; 2 Thes. 1:6–10). Non-

Dispensationalist Pre-Millennialists (e.g., George Eldon Ladd)[163] hold this view.[164]

Amillennialism teaches that the "millennial" reign of Christ is his present, invisible rule enthroned at the right hand of the Father in heaven. The Second Coming, then, will *end* Christ's reign, not begin it. Paul seems to see things this way in 1 Corinthians 15:24–28. St. Augustine held this view, too. The Tribulation and the Antichrist would appear *after* the millennium. How do Amillennialists deal with Revelation 20? They spiritualize it, pointing to the heavily symbolic character of the book. So how do Pre-Millennialists deal with 1 Corinthians 15:24–28? They see it as describing the end of the Millennium, which they read in between verses 23 and 24, taking the "then" of verse 24 to imply a subsequent stage (quite a gulp!). Catholic, Reformed, and Lutheran Churches are Amillennialist.

Post-Millennialism: Called "the eschatology of victory," this view rejects the apocalyptic Pre-Millennialist expectation that history will spiral downward till the intervention of God. Instead, they believe, history will become "his story." At the end of the age the influence of the Holy Spirit or the "leaven of the gospel" will permeate the world, ushering in a golden age of peace and salvation, at the end of which Christ will return to a kingdom prepared for him. (See the parables of gradual growth, Mark 4:30–32; Matthew 13:33). This was the doctrine of the Puritans. It was also embraced by the Holiness Revival of the nineteenth century, from whence it passed on into the Social Gospel Movement, albeit in a demythologized form, minus the expectation of a literal Second Coming of Christ.

---

163. George Eldon Ladd, *The Blessed Hope: A Biblical Study of the Second Advent and the Rapture* (Grand Rapids: Eerdmans, 1956).

164. Robert Gundry, *The Church and the Tribulation* (Grand Rapids: Zondervan, 1973).

Realized Eschatology: Disappointing Results

Mark's gospel presupposes the same crisis actuating John 21:23 and 2 Peter 3:3–10: the death of the first generation of the disciples. Note the "tree rings" in the Markan trunk. Mark 13:30 has Jesus promise the End would arrive before the contemporary generation had passed away. But it didn't pan out, so an editor added verses 32–33 in order to retract the original promise. But that's not all. Someone has added the break-flow of verses 7–8 in exactly the same spirit as 2 Thessalonians 2:1–12, which throws a wet blanket on apocalyptic fervor by stipulating several events that must transpire before the End comes. Subsequently, someone added Mark 13:10, which stretches out the timetable long enough to allow for world evangelization! Most of the Jesus-generation were dead by the time Mark wrote the Transfiguration narrative, which he places immediately after 9:1, another prediction of an early Parousia with an important modification: now it is only "some" of those present who will live to see the big event. This is presumably the reason he has only Peter, James, and John accompany Jesus up the mountain to see him transfigured. Otherwise, what's wrong with the other nine? It seems pretty clear, then, that Mark has nominated the Transfiguration as a replacement for the promised (but failed) Parousia. As if to say, "Okay, it's not the actual kingdom of God, but it's better than nothing, right?"

Luke did the same thing a different way. He subtly alters the Mark 9:1 promise, "Some standing here will not taste death before they see the kingdom of God come with power." Luke's version omits "with power" (Luke 9:27), implying it will not after all be a Technicolor Apocalypse, the very point of Luke 17:20–21: "The kingdom of God is not coming with observable signs, nor will they say, 'Here it is!' or 'There!' For the kingdom of God is within you." Not only this, but Luke adds new material to the parable of the Talents/Minas (Luke 19:11–27), which he pre-interprets for the reader: "he proceeded to tell a parable . . . because they supposed that the kingdom of God was to appear immediately." In other words, "Whoa! Not so fast!" And of course you realize this is not actually Jesus correcting his fans but rather Luke correcting his readers.

By the time the Johannine Appendix was stapled onto the end of John chapter 20, the original conclusion, the last known survivor of "this generation" *had* passed away. So somebody figured the only retreat left was to reinterpret the promise/prediction as purely hypothetical. But originally, the Fourth Evangelist, "John," had taken a far different, and far more radical approach: "Realized eschatology." Suppose the kingdom of God *did* come, but secretly, invisibly. What if you had to have the awakened eye of faith to see it (John 3:3)? In John 6:25 Jesus declares, "Truly, truly I say to you, the hour is coming, *and now is*, when the dead will hear the voice of the Son of God, and those who hear will live." Our Ecclesiastical Redactor was not at liberty simply to cut this verse, but he attempted to negate it, adding a more orthodox-sounding paraphrase only a few verses later: "Do not marvel at this, for the hour is coming when all *who are in the tombs* will hear his voice and come forth, those who have done good, to the resurrection of life, and those who have done evil to the resurrection of judgment" (John 5:28–29).

See the difference? In the first passage, the "dead" are the spiritually dead, but if they "hear" (i.e., realize the truth of) the Redeemer's preaching, and not all will, they will find themselves spiritually resurrected. But the second speaks of the literal resurrection of the literally dead, the rotting dead, good and bad. The first envisions the present, the second the future. In other words, someone did not like the abandonment of traditional, futuristic eschatology and decided he'd better restore it!

Likewise, in John 14:22, Judas (not the Betrayer) realizes that something has changed: "Lord, how is it that you will manifest yourself to us, and *not to the world*?" Jesus explains that the Parousia will take place *inside* them (just as in Luke 17:20–21): "If a man loves me, he will keep my word, and my Father will love him, and we will come to him and make our home with him." Forget about "every eye will see him"!

Obviously, this is the tried-and-true(?) strategy of making virtue of necessity. It saves face, since one hides behind the pretence that Realized Eschatology is more "spiritual," more sophisticated than stupid, childish literal eschatology. But ultimately it becomes apparent that the world has not changed, nor have believers, in any discernible way. Just think of certain Christmas carols in this light: "Joy to the earth! The Saviour reigns!" Uh, how can you tell? "He rules the world with truth and grace and makes the nations prove [i.e., attest] the glories of his righteousness and wonders of his love!" Really? How did I miss that? Jürgen Moltmann said,

> Christian theology must show how far the Christian confession of faith in Jesus is true as seen from the outside, and must demonstrate that it is relevant to the present-day understanding of reality and the present-day dispute about the truth of God and the righteousness of man and the world. For the title "Christ" has never been used by faith only to say who Jesus was in his own person, but to express his dominion, future and significance with regard to God, men, and the world.[165]

Given the grandiose claim implied in the title, how it pertains to world-transformation, it *has* to be relevant to the public world, or the whole thing's a joke. Once I sat as a guest in a Baha'i meeting commemorating the historic day on which Mullah Hussein recognized Mirza Ali Muhammad as the Bab ("Gate"), the earthly spokesman for the Hidden Imam of the Shi'ites. A young man present exclaimed: How different would the world be today had Hussein not had the insight to discern the Bab's identity! I could not help think-

165. Jürgen Moltmann, *The Crucified God: The Cross of Christ as the Foundation and Criticism of Christian Theology.* Trans. R.A. Wilson and John Bowden (New York: Harper & Row, 1974), p. 84.

ing, "Yeah? How different *is* the world because of it?"

Well, it's undeniable that the world is different today because the Christ did *not* arrive as promised. As Freud might have said, this trauma, desperately repressed via reinterpretation, caused a mass historical neurosis for Christians forever after. Just as the repressed trauma of an individual keeps tapping him on the shoulder via dreams, psychogenetic symptoms, and verbal slips, urging the neurotic to face the festering trauma and deal with it, Christians are momentarily bothered and puzzled when their eyes happen upon passages like Mark 13:30. But still they dare not face the trauma. They cannot allow themselves to recognize the delay of the Parousia and its disastrous implications as Reimarus did.

Neuroses tend to lock the sufferer into a pattern of repeating the trauma again and again, by leading him to view new events through the lens of the traumatic past, causing history to repeat itself. In just this fashion does the unacknowledged trauma of the failed Second Coming cause Christians in every generation to recalculate "the day and the hour," only to be disappointed and embarrassed every time. I use the word "disappointed" rather than "disillusioned" because they never seem to learn the lesson. Let's just buy another lottery ticket! And until the trump of Gabriel does finally sound, we can just keep indulging in "Rapture porn," all those awful movies and novels depicting the Antichrist, the Rapture, etc.

Conclusion

What does Paul mean in 1 Corinthians 2:1–5? He may be telling us more than he realizes.

> When I came to you, brethren, I did not come proclaiming to you the testimony of God in lofty words or wisdom. For I decided to know nothing among you except Jesus Christ and him crucified. And I was with you in weakness and in much fear and trem-

bling; and my speech and my message were not in plausible words of wisdom, but in demonstration of the Spirit and of power, that your faith might not rest in the wisdom of men but in the power of God.

He is revealing something about communication and convincement. When he speaks of "demonstration of the Spirit and of power," he is putting in theological terms what I should describe as the appeal to emotion. He says that in his recruitment efforts he eschewed the strategy of attempting to convince the Corinthians by logical argumentation ("plausible words of wisdom"). Why? Because, had he succeeded in that approach, the faith of the Corinthians would be vulnerable, fickle. If some sophist came along next month with what seemed better arguments, the Corinthians might as easily drop their Christian allegiance for a new one. Their sails would have remained set to catch "every wind of doctrine" (Eph. 4:14). They'd have had "itching ears" (2 Tim. 4:3), like the Athenian dilettantes ever eager to hear some new idea or speculation (Acts 17: 19–21). No, Paul knew that an emotional "convincement" (if you can even call it that) was likely more permanent. Resting as it does on emotion, it cannot easily succumb to rational argumentation, since it is not founded upon rational arguments.

But might that not be appropriate? One does not fall in love by rational calculus. It is not like shopping for a car on the basis of your dog-eared copy of *Consumer Reports*. No, it is *not* appropriate if the thing you are deciding to believe out of emotions, or because you like the sound of it, entails assertions about what happened in the past, e.g., a resurrection on the third day or creation of the world in six days. That is a cheating short-cut.

But C.S. Lewis bids us take it. In his essay, "On Obstinacy in Belief" he argues that the commitment to faith in God must remain inviolable and invulnerable to contrary evidence once the commitment is made because it is like getting married or sealing a friendship, forming a personal relationship of loyal trust with another. From then on, "love believes all things."

> What would, a moment before, have been variations in opinion, now become variations in your personal attitude to a Person. You are no longer faced with an argument which demands your assent, but with a Person who demands your confidence.[166]

But how do we know there *is* such a "Person"? I'm afraid it boils down to this: if you want to remain "loyal" to a belief in God, you have to resolve to close your eyes to new evidence or arguments that, had you known them back when you were weighing the evidence as to whether to believe in God or not, might have caused you to reject that belief. Lewis *is* talking about stubbornness of belief. He has said, albeit in typically charming language, that his mind is made up; please don't confuse him with the facts.

Morris Goldstein[167] shows how fifteenth-century Jewish philosopher Joseph Albo raised the same issue.

> A pertinent question of interest to the modern reader is the one introduced in Chapter 24 of Book I in *Sefer Ha-Ikkarim* [The Book of Principles]. May, or should, one investigate his own religion to see whether it is true? May he adopt another religion if it appears to be truer? Here is Albo's answer. Investigation shows doubt; where there is doubt there can be no firm belief; reward for belief will be found only when it is firm and doubt-free. On the second part of the question, whether one should investigate another religion and accept it when it seems to be truer, his reply is that one may learn of a third religion and on investigation be won to *it*; this could continue until one has examined *every* religion, but he

---

166. C.S. Lewis, "On Obstinacy in Belief." In Lewis, *The World's Last Night and other Essays*. A Harvest Book (San Diego: Harcourt, 1987), p. 26.

167. Goldstein, *Jesus in the Jewish Tradition*, p. 213.

can never be satisfied, for there may be a still truer religion which is unknown to him; hence doubt will remain and he will not be saved by his belief.

The great Anglo-Irish fantasiste Edward John Moreton Drax Plunkett, 18th Baron of Dunsany (or just "Lord Dunsany"), wrote a story that seems to me to communicate the point at issue better than any didactic prose can.

THE SORROW OF SEARCH[168]

It is told also of King Khanazar how he bowed very low unto the gods of Old. None bowed so low unto the gods of Old as did King Khanazar.

One day the King returning from the worship of the gods of Old and from bowing before them in the temple of the gods commanded their prophets to appear before him, saying:

"I would know somewhat concerning the gods."

Then came the prophets before King Khanazar, burdened with many books, to whom the King said:

"It is not in books."

Thereat the prophets departed, bearing away with them a thousand methods well devised in books whereby men may gain wisdom of the gods. One alone remained, a master prophet, who had forgotten books, to whom the King said:

"The gods of Old are mighty."

And answered the master prophet:

"Very mighty are the gods of Old."

Then said the King:

"There are no gods but the gods of Old."

And answered the prophet:

"There are none other."

And they two being alone within the palace the King said:

"Tell me aught concerning gods or men if aught of the truth be known."

---

168. *Time and the Gods*, by Lord Dunsany, [1905], at sacred-texts.com

Then said the master prophet:

"Far and white and straight lieth the road to Knowing, and down it in the heat and dust go all wise people of the earth, but in the fields before they come to it the very wise lie down or pluck the flowers. By the side of the road to Knowing—O King, it is hard and hot—stand many temples, and in the doorway of every temple stand many priests, and they cry to the travellers that weary of the road, crying to them:

"This is the End."

And in the temples are the sounds of music, and from each roof arises the savour of pleasant burning; and all that look at a cool temple, whichever temple they look at, or hear the hidden music, turn in to see whether it be indeed the End. And such as find that their temple is not indeed the End set forth again upon the dusty road, stopping at each temple as they pass for fear they miss the End, or striving onwards on the road, and see nothing in the dust, till they can walk no longer and are taken worn and weary of their journey into some other temple by a kindly priest who shall tell them that this also is the End. Neither on that road may a man gain any guiding from his fellows, for only one thing that they say is surely true, when they say:

"Friend, we can see nothing for the dust."

And of the dust that hides the way much has been there since ever that road began, and some is stirred up by the feet of all that travel upon it, and more arises from the temple doors.

And, O King, it were better for thee, travelling upon that road, to rest when thou hearest one calling: "This is the End," with the sounds of music behind him. And if in the dust and darkness thou pass by Lo and Mush and the pleasant temple of Kynash, or Sheenath with his opal smile, or Sho with his eyes of agate, yet Shilo and Mynarthitep, Gazo and Amurund and Slig are still before thee and the priests of their temples will not forget to call thee.

And, O King, it is told that only one discerned the end and passed by three thousand temples, and the priests of the last were like the priests of the first, and all said that their temple was at the end of the road, and the dark of the dust lay over them all, and all were very pleasant and only the road was weary. And in some were many gods, and in a few only one, and in some the shrine was empty, and all had many priests, and in all the travellers were happy as they rested. And into some his fellow travellers tried to force him, and when he said:

"I will travel further," many said:

"This man lies, for the road ends here."

And he that travelled to the End hath told that when the thunder was heard upon the road there arose the sound of the voices of all the priests as far as he could hear, crying:

"Hearken to Shilo"—"Hear Mush"—"Lo! Kynash"—"The voice of Sho"— "Mynarthitep is angry"—"Hear the word of Slig!"

And far away along the road one cried to the traveller that Sheenath stirred in his sleep.

O King this is very doleful. It is told that that traveller came at last to the utter End and there was a mighty gulf, and in the darkness at the bottom of the gulf one small god crept, no bigger than a hare, whose voice came crying in the cold:

"I know not."

And beyond the gulf was nought, only the small god crying.

And he that travelled to the End fled backwards for a great distance till he came to temples again, and entering one where a priest cried:

"This is the End," lay down and rested on a couch. There Yush sat silent, carved with an emerald tongue and two great eyes of sapphire, and there many rested and were happy. And an old priest, coming from comforting a child, came over to that traveller who had seen the End and said to him:

"This is Yush and this is the End of wisdom."

And the traveller answered:

"Yush is very peaceful and this indeed the End."

"O King, wouldst thou hear more?"

And the King said:

"I would hear all."

And the master prophet answered:

"There was also another prophet and his name was Shaun, who had such reverence for the gods of Old that he became able to discern their forms by starlight as they strode, unseen by others, among men. Each night did Shaun discern the forms of the gods and every day he taught concerning them, till men in Averon knew how the gods appeared all grey against the mountains, and how Rhoog was higher than Mount Scagadon, and how Skun was smaller, and how Asgool leaned forward as he strode, and how Trodath peered about him with small eyes. But one night as Shaun watched the gods of Old by starlight, he faintly discerned some other gods that sat far up the slopes of the mountains in the stillness behind the gods of Old. And the next day he hurled his robe away that he wore as Averon's prophet and said to his people:

"There be gods greater than the gods of Old, three gods seen faintly on the hills by starlight looking on Averon."

And Shaun set out and travelled many days and many people followed him. And every night he saw more clearly the shapes of the three new gods who sat silent when the gods of Old were striding among men. On the higher slopes of the mountain Shaun stopped with all his people, and there they built a city and worshipped the gods, whom only Shaun could see, seated above them on the mountain. And Shaun taught how the gods were like grey streaks of light seen before dawn, and how the god on the right pointed upward toward the sky, and how the god on the left pointed downward toward the ground, but the god in the middle slept.

And in the city Shaun's followers built three temples. The one on the right was a temple for the young, and the one on the left a temple for the old, and the third was a temple with doors closed and barred—therein none ever entered. One night as Shaun watched before the three gods sitting like pale light against the mountain, he saw on the mountain's summit two gods that spake together and pointed, mocking the gods of the hill, only he heard no sound. The next day Shaun set out and a few followed him to climb to the mountain's summit in the cold, to find the gods who were so great that they mocked at the silent three. And near the two gods they halted and built for themselves huts. Also they built a temple wherein the Two were carved by the hand of Shaun with their heads turned towards each other, with mockery on Their faces and Their fingers pointing, and beneath Them were carved the three gods of the hill as actors making sport. None remembered now Asgool, Trodath, Skun, and Rhoog, the gods of Old.

For many years Shaun and his few followers lived in their huts upon the mountain's summit worshipping gods that mocked, and every night Shaun saw the two gods by starlight as they laughed to one another in the silence. And Shaun grew old.

One night as his eyes were turned towards the Two, he saw across the mountains in the distance a great god seated in the plain and looming enormous to the sky, who looked with angry eyes towards the Two as they sat and mocked. Then said Shaun to his people, the few that had followed him thither:

"Alas that we may not rest, but beyond us in the plain sitteth the one true god and he is wroth with mocking. Let us therefore leave these two that sit and mock and let us find the truth in the worship of that greater god, who even though he kill shall yet not mock us."

But the people answered:

"Thou hast taken from us many gods and taught us now to worship gods that mock, and if there is laughter on their faces as we die, lo! thou alone canst see it, and we would rest."

But three men who had grown old with following followed still.

And down the steep mountain on the further side Shaun led them, saying:

"Now we shall surely know."

And the three old men answered:

"We shall know indeed, O last of all the prophets."

That night the two gods mocking at their worshippers mocked not at Shaun nor his three followers, who coming to the plain still travelled on till they came at last to a place where the eyes of Shaun at night could closely see the vast form of their god. And beyond them as far as the sky there lay a marsh. There they rested, building such shelters as they could, and said to one another:

"This is the End, for Shaun discerneth that there are no more gods, and before us lieth the marsh and old age hath come upon us."

And since they could not labour to build a temple, Shaun carved upon a rock all that he saw by starlight of the great god of the plain; so that if ever others forsook the gods of Old because they saw beyond them the Greater Three, and should thence come to knowledge of the Twain that mocked, and should yet persevere in wisdom till they saw by starlight him whom Shaun named the Ultimate god, they should still find there upon the rock what one had written concerning the end of search. For three years Shaun carved upon the rock, and rising one night from carving, saying:

"Now is my labour done," saw in the distance four greater gods beyond the Ultimate god. Proudly in the distance beyond the marsh these gods were tramping together, taking no heed of the god upon the plain. Then said Shaun to his three followers:

"Alas that we know not yet, for there be gods beyond the marsh."

None would follow Shaun, for they said that old age must end all quests, and that they would rather wait there in the plain for Death than that he should pursue them across the marsh.

Then Shaun said farewell to his followers, saying:

"You have followed me well since ever we forsook the gods of Old to worship greater gods. Farewell. It may be that your prayers at evening shall avail when you pray to the god of the plain, but I must go onward, for there be gods beyond."

So Shaun went down into the marsh, and for three days struggled through it, and on the third night saw the four gods not very far away, yet could not discern Their faces. All the next day Shaun toiled on to see Their faces by starlight, but ere the night came up or one star shone, at set of sun, Shaun fell down before the feet of his four gods. The stars came out, and the faces of the four shone bright and clear, but Shaun saw them not, for the labour of toiling and seeing was over for Shaun; and lo! They were Asgool, Trodath, Skun, and Rhoog—The gods of Old.

Then said the King:

"It is well that the sorrow of search cometh only to the wise, for the wise are very few."

Also the King said:

"Tell me this thing, O prophet. Who are the true gods?"

The master prophet answered:

"Let the King command."

* * *

One begins to see the wisdom of Paul Tillich's understanding of *faith as ultimate concern*. Faith, he explains, is not the opposite of doubt except in the sense that it is the *yin* to doubt's *yang*. Faith is Jacob wrestling with the angel, Antonius Block demanding answers from the Grim Reaper who confesses he is just as much in the dark. It is Jesus in Gethsemane, Abraham agonizing over God's terrible command. Faith is the journey, not a premature stop mistaken for a destination. Once you see this, you will no more be disappointed. You will realize that your inherited belief is not the Ultimate Truth, but merely Christianity.

About the Author

Robert M. Price is the host of the podcasts The Bible Geek and The Human Bible, as well as the author of many books. He is the founder and editor of the *Journal of Higher Criticism*.